Praise for *It's the Customer, Stupid!*

"There's no need to buy a dozen books on customer service. Just buy one—this one! Michael Aun gets to the heart of what it takes to win and keep today's demanding customer."

—**Joe Calloway author of** *Becoming a Category of One*

"Michael Aun is terrific on and off the platform . . . entertaining and educating! He's excelled himself in this magnificent book."

—**Ed Foreman, U. S. Congressman (Retired), Texas and New Mexico**

"Success in business is all about loyal and happy customers. Michael Aun is a genius when it comes to customer relationships. Use his ideas and you will find success."

—**Jeff Slutsky, author of** *Street Fighter Marketing Solutions*

"Michael Aun is right *aun* target with this *ausome* book, and the one thing *aul* businesses forget—to *auways* focus *aun* the customer. Right *aun*, Aun!"

—**Ronald P. Culberson, MSW, CSP, Humorist and author of** *Is Your Glass Laugh Full* **and** *My Kneecap Seems Too Loose*

"Michael Aun describes why your most important goals are your customers' goals; how sold customers can become your most abused customers; and why keeping current customers is easier than developing new ones."

—**Dr. Larry Baker, CSP; Internationally Known Management Consultant, Coach, Speaker, Author, and Publisher**

"Michael Aun is the king of customer service! Master the fine art of impeccable customer service that leads to loyalty and trust through his masterful ideas. This book is packed with ideas, concepts, and testaments that will transform the way you operate your business."

—**Dr. Nido Qubein, President, High Point University; Chairman, Great Harvest Bread Co.**

"Astounding customer service is the best strategy for competing in today's marketplace. Being on par in terms of price and quality only gets you into the game, astounding customer service wins the game. *It's the Customer, Stupid!* is the blueprint for exceeding customer expectations and creating lifetime customers who are raving fans."

—**Dr. Tony Alessandra, author of**
The NEW Art of Managing People
and *The Platinum Rule*

"Michael Aun's newest book gets to the point very quickly: Focus on your customers needs. Listen, listen, listen, and then listen some more. Great wisdom can be mined in 34 chapters. Buy this book! Read this book! And apply the time-valued rules. It's a winner!"

—**Dr. Peter Legge, OBC, CSP, CPAE; Author,**
Businessman, and Professional Speaker

"Michael Aun's *It's the Customer, Stupid!* will inspire you to find opportunities to build your business with the wisdom from a man who knows how to do it. Be *smart* and read this book!"

—**Giovanni Livera, President, TimeCompass,**
Inc.; author of *Live A Thousand Years*

"Michael Aun provides extraordinarily wise counsel for everyone smart enough to follow his advice for positively impacting customers. Anyone who desires to remove the 'bag filled with stupid customer activities' will be wise to embrace Michael Aun's proven strategies of providing lifetime service to all customers and clients. Based on his successful career of attracting, serving, and keeping customers, Michael Aun offers 34 profound ways to engage his customer based success. As we say, 'Listening Pays in Many Ways!,' and the wise will listen to Michael Aun."

—**Dr. Lyman K. "Manny" Steil, CEO, International**
Listening Leadership Institute; author
of *Listening Leaders: The Ten Golden*
Rules to Listen, Lead and Succeed

IT'S THE CUSTOMER, STUPID!

IT'S THE CUSTOMER, STUPID!

34

Wake-up calls to help you stay client-focused

MICHAEL AUN

WILEY

John Wiley & Sons, Inc.

Published by John Wiley & Sons, Inc., Hoboken, New Jersey.
Published simultaneously in Canada.

For general information on our other products and services or for technical support, please contact our Customer Care Department within the United States at (800) 762-2974, outside the United States at (317) 572-3993 or fax (317) 572-4002.

Wiley also publishes its books in a variety of electronic formats. Some content that appears in print may not be available in electronic books. For more information about Wiley products, visit our web site at www.wiley.com.

Library of Congress Cataloging-in-Publication Data:

Aun, Michael, 1949-

   It's the customer, stupid! : 34 wake-up calls to help you stay client-focused/Michael Aun.
       p. cm.
   Includes index.
   ISBN 978-0-470-90739-9 (cloth)
   ISBN 978-1-118-00126-4 (ebk)
   ISBN 978-1-118-00127-1 (ebk)
   ISBN 978-1-118-00128-8 (ebk)
       1. Customer services.   2. Customer relations—Management.   I. Title.
   HF5415.5.A96   2011
   658.8'12—dc22

                                                          2010034667

Printed in the United States of America
10 9 8 7 6 5 4 3 2 1

CONTENTS

FOREWORD

MICHAEL SHARES HIS WEALTH

In today's "What's in it for me right now?" world, Michael Aun stands as a successful person who recognizes that "right now" is not as powerful as "day-by-day." Consistency wins the race. And consistency is only one of Michael's success attributes. Family man, high ethics, and dogmatic to achieve and be positive from the first minute of the morning until his head hits the pillow at night, are some others.

His engaging online publication, "Behind the Mike," is a misnomer. Michael Aun is always out in front. It's the reason he has achieved so much in his career, and it's the reason he will continue to achieve. I always read it from beginning to end. It's loaded with insight, humor, and wisdom.

In this book, *It's the Customer, Stupid!*, Michael goes to great lengths to explain the validity and the monetary value of customers, repeat customers, loyal customers, and referred customers. Because everyone is looking to make sales, build business, increase profits, and become successful *now*, this book addresses the gold in your own backyard that you are not mining. Your customers. Better stated, your loyal customers.

Michael has succeeded in the insurance business, which in my opinion is the most difficult business to achieve over the long term. In a market segment where no one wants to meet with the seller, Michael was always able to meet with the buyer, and he didn't just make sales, he established relationships and over the years has kept a fiercely loyal customer base. Not just renewals, but also referrals.

In this book Michael explains the why, the how, and the how much. Think about your own customer base or your own client base.

How do they feel about you?

How do they talk about you?

What do they mean to you? (But more important, what do you mean to them?)

How valuable are you?

How believable are you?

How available are you?

And how trustworthy are you perceived to be?

All of these qualities ensure success, but not one without the other. And all of these qualities are Michael Aun qualities.

Everyone—including you—is looking for *today's* answers. An idea, a direction, a plan. This book is loaded with them. He's not saying, "Go back to basics." He's saying, "Here are the fundamentals. Here's how I handled them, here's how I mastered them, and here's what you need to do. Now!"

We're living in a time of doubt, a time of uncertainty, and a time of distrust. This book provides a road map for gaining these critical fundamental attributes while others are losing them.

NOTE WELL: As you read this book you would be well advised to grab a highlighter, read slowly, and make notes in the margins. And if you are persistent enough, and consistent enough, to turn those notes into actions, then you will have maximized the value of this book.

It's funny, when I first saw the title of this book, I immediately thought about how many companies I have talked to, and how many people, especially salespeople and service people, I have spoken with. When they talk about customers they say, "It's the stupid customer!"

Blaming is so easy in this world at this time. Taking responsibility is so much harder. But believe it or not it's safer, and more rewarding, for both the customer and for you.

Everyone has an idea, philosophy, or strategy about what customers are all about. Michael Aun has a passion for what customers are all about. And as you look through the table of contents you will find that he also has an *understanding* of what customers are all about.

It is from his lifetime of experience that you will gain new insights about the critical customer service topics in today's markets, including word-of-mouth marketing, word-of-mouth advertising, finding out what the customer really thinks, giving the customer more than they were expecting, having a service heart, problem resolution, and the all-important skills of communication.

As a high-level Toastmaster, Michael has mastered the art and the science of communicating to a group and an individual, as husband and wife or a thousand husbands and wives.

This book also tackles the sensitive subjects of taking responsibility, advocacy, time management, speed of response, and bad news.

The cool part about bad news is that Michael shows you how to turn it into great news and provides insight that will help you understand how bad news occurs, how fast it travels, and the magic of converting it to good news.

As if all this weren't enough, there is the sensitive topic of results (or should I say measuring results). Michael's leadership both demands results and commands results. Michael's style and leadership ensure results and do it using the voice of his customer, included with his own it is those collaborative qualities.

He doesn't "have" customers; he has fiercely loyal customers. They are an integral part of his success and Michael shows you how to make them an integral part of yours.

This book delivers Michael's experience as a salesman, a manager, a speaker, a businessman, a husband, a father, a grandfather, and a person of character. It's authentic. And Michael's authenticity is transferable—to you.

I've known Michael for nearly 20 years. We are fellow members of the National Speakers Association Hall of Fame. In fact, he was the one who nominated me. In order to respect someone's words and honor someone's deeds, you have to respect the person, and Michael Aun is the shining example of what to do in business, in family, and in life.

Jeffrey Gitomer
Author of *The Little Red Book of Selling*

ACKNOWLEDGMENTS

Special thanks have to be given to Toastmasters International and my local Osceola Club 1841 in Kissimmee, Florida, and especially Nancy Street, who helped edit this manuscript. Without Toastmasters, my entire business and speaking career would not have been possible.

I want to thank my family as well. My late parents, Alice and Michael Aun, brought 11 children into this world and nurtured them with good habits and discipline. Any success I have enjoyed in my life is a by-product of their love, care, and encouragement.

I want to thank the most incredible salespeople on the planet, my extraordinary granddaughters, Ashley and Ava, who are only four and two at the time this goes to press. They are the greatest salespeople I have ever known, masterful at asking questions and never taking "no" for answer. Neither have a clue what the word "no" means. They do understand the power of "why?"

The most important people in my life are my wife, Christine, and our three sons, Cory, Jason, and Christopher. I learned many great principles from my amazing sons. The students became the teachers.

Jason, who is a microbiologist, taught me the incredible power of self-discipline as he and his twin brother, Cory, became national champion weightlifters.

Cory taught me the importance of being a mentor and coach for other people. He is an astonishing athletic coach and teacher of biology and the sciences. He brings fun and education into his classroom and onto

XVIII   ACKNOWLEDGMENTS

the playing fields, helping children to love the sciences and athletics. His fellow coaches and teachers as well as his students and athletes sing his praises, which is a powerful customer service testimonial.

My youngest son, Christopher, taught me the noteworthy gift of "giving" by providing care for others. Like his mother, he is a registered nurse. The nature of that profession is the greatest testimonial to customer service that exists. He inspires me with the good work he and other medical professionals do every day.

I am also moved by the good works done by the medical staff of the St. Thomas Aquinas Free Medical Clinic in my church in St. Cloud, Florida. The 75 doctors and 150 nurses and other volunteers donate their time, talent, and treasure so that the poor can have health care; that is truly a remarkable tribute to what servant leadership is all about.

Finally and most importantly, I want to thank the most important person in my life, my wonderful wife, Christine. She has taught me how to love and care for others though it might not always be easy to do so. She always admonishes me to "Be nice and everything else takes care of itself." She never had one day of customer service training, but in my mind, she knows more about caring for a customer than any person I have ever met. She is the true motivation for *It's the Customer, Stupid!* and is the reason for any success it will enjoy. I love her more than life itself.

God bless all who have touched my life to make this book possible.

CHAPTER 1

UNHAPPY CUSTOMERS WILL NOT ONLY FIRE YOU BUT THEY WILL TELL OTHERS!

Dissatisfied customers tell an average of 10 other people about their bad experience. Twelve percent tell up to 20 people.

Every company on the planet talks about rendering dynamite customer service. Some like to refer to their customer service departments as "Customer Care Centers." Ironically, however, the cuffs often don't match the collar. Although these organizations espouse the great respect they have for their clients, they build multiple walls around the company to prevent these very customers from getting a fair shake.

While I'm amazed by the hypocritical attitude that seems to pervade much of the corporate world today, I'm not surprised when corporate culture asks customers: "What have you done for me lately?" Their mission statement espouses one thing; their actual *mission* does quite another.

The term "customer satisfaction" may be too subjective and impossible to define. Why? As it is with beauty, it is defined by the buyer, not the seller. Indeed, most corporate cultures couldn't care less what their buyers think. After all, just look at the way they treat them.

First, they assume that most customers are trying to find "something for nothing." Second, they make the client wait on hold for unreasonable periods of time before grandly coming on the phone line to ask how they can "be of help." Third, they build impossible barriers that the client is forced to navigate to garner any "satisfaction." Finally, the client must play by *their* rules to get any kind of results. No wonder clients are wary of the empty promise of "customer satisfaction."

The fact is that keeping customers "satisfied" simply isn't enough anymore. In fact, if they're merely satisfied, they often don't bother to come back—because they don't like the rules by which they had to play in order to attain this "satisfaction." And if this is the sorry way most satisfied customers treat you, imagine how ticked off the genuinely *dissatisfied* customer is.

The unhappy customer will tell an average of 10 other people about their bad experience. Twelve percent will tell up to 20 people. To that end, it's not enough to simply satisfy a customer anymore. Satisfaction is a 3 on a scale of 1 to 10—and it simply won't do.

You have to promise a lot nowadays, but you have to deliver more. And whatever you do promise, you must *absolutely* deliver.

Case in point: There is a Domino's Pizza vendor in south Detroit who receives the same phone call every Thursday afternoon from someone ordering a hamburger, mushroom, and onion pizza at 4:30 PM By 5:00 PM or thereabouts, Domino's delivers the pizza. At 5:30 PM the same customer calls back and complains that he was unhappy with the pizza, and before 6:00 PM on Thursday afternoon of each week, Domino's refunds this customer his money.

To be fair, the customer is simply taking advantage of the Domino's promise. But Domino's *made* the promise. In fact, Domino's built its entire company on a promise. In the early days, if they failed to deliver within 30 minutes, you got the pizza for free. Then a huge lawsuit ensued that prompted the chain to alter its promise. However, Domino's still stands by its product today—and if you don't like it, you don't pay.

I asked a Domino's vendor once what this promise cost his shop over the course of a year. "Maybe around $200," he replied. "[But] the well-publicized stories [on the company] done by *60 Minutes* and other [television shows] . . . have been estimated to be worth tens of millions of dollars in free advertising." Keeping customers happy pays dividends.

It is the customer's opinion of the bad news, stupid—and it travels faster today than ever before.

TAKEAWAY SERVICING AND SELLING TACTICS

1. Unhappy customers will fire you on the spot because they now have options that will only increase.
2. They won't just fire you; unhappy clients will personally tell up to 10 people about their bad experience. Twelve percent will tell 20 people.

CHAPTER 2

GREAT CUSTOMER SERVICE IS ABOUT GETTING THE CLIENT'S FEEDBACK

Happy customers will tell an average of five people about their positive experience.

I'm blessed to be married to the most patient person in the world. My wife, Christine, is the perfect customer. She genuinely feels that the company always deserves the benefit of the doubt and goes to great pains to give them the opportunity to fix a problem when one exists.

Christine patiently navigates her way through the corporate maze that companies construct to render achieving customer satisfaction something of an oxymoron for most of us mere mortals. And when she finally gets what she was after, she's so appreciative that she writes glowing testimonials to the same people who gave her the third degree to get there—all for doing simply what they are *supposed* to do. After all, she's a customer; she paid for the product or service.

I, on the other hand, have a short fuse. I want what I paid for from the beginning and I don't want to beg. In fact, the title of my most popular keynote address on customer service is "Have I Gotta Beg to Buy?" Laugh at it if you will, but the fact is most customers feel this

5

way about the whole buying process. They'd rather milk a cobra than wander through this maze.

I've spoken on this topic at least 75 to 100 times a year for almost four decades, and nearly every single presentation is different. I do up to 50 hours of interviews with every client to find out what they think the issues are. Ironically, the most revealing interviews come from the client's own customer, whom I also interview.

Mind you, I go into those interviews knowing that they are going to steer me toward a happy customer who is an ongoing client. Even the happy ones have a laundry list of things they were expecting but did not receive.

Though one might wonder why this is, the answer is probably simpler than you think. Maybe, just maybe, the folks charged with the responsibility of sales, marketing, and customer service weren't trained any better, or maybe they weren't selected properly. You can hire an idiot and "train" him or her, but all you end up with is a well-trained idiot. The fault may well lie in many different areas of the process.

TAKE A LESSON FROM MILLIKEN & COMPANY

In my opinion, the greatest company on the planet is textile giant Milliken & Company, based out of Spartanburg, South Carolina. Since winning the World Championship of Public Speaking for Toastmasters in 1978, I have had the privilege of addressing thousands of audiences in some 22 countries throughout the world. Milliken is my favorite group because they think differently—which makes them a champion in the textile business.

Milliken provides better customer service than any company I know of for a variety of reasons. First and foremost, they require all employees to complete 40 hours of continuing education per year, just to keep their jobs. The company pays for their employees' courses and offers a variety of choices from Toastmasters to their famous POE weekends, an acronym for Pursuit of Excellence. For years, I had the opportunity to address dozens of Milliken's POE conferences throughout the Carolinas and Georgia, working alongside speaking giants Tom Peters and others.

GREAT CUSTOMER SERVICE IS ABOUT GREAT TRAINING

According to industry standards, Milliken is not the highest paid workforce in the textile industry. However, some would argue that they are the best trained in the world. Milliken believes you have to teach people to think differently and creatively. Their mantra is simple: To do it better, you have to do it differently.

When I was first introduced to Milliken, I learned of their now-renowned ECR Program, another of their famous acronyms, which stands for *Error Cause Removal*. Unlike most of their peers, Milliken encourages creative thinking—and they back it up with cash. Milliken managers prowl the floors of their plants, encouraging their employees to find a better way to do a project.

Any new ideas that employees imagine do not go into a suggestion box to be opened three years later. Rather, employees are encouraged to step up and voice their ideas on the spot. Ideas that have merit are implemented immediately. The employee receives a cash bonus that the manager has been empowered to reward. The net result is that Milliken has one of the most innovative workforces in the worldwide textile corridor, with employees who are the envy of the international textile community.

YOU GET THE BEHAVIOR YOU REWARD

Milliken realizes an important trend: You get the behavior you reward. The longer it takes to recognize good habits, the less likely employees are to engage in them.

DURING MY CAREER AS A MOTIVATIONAL SPEAKER, I HAVE LEARNED THREE INCONTROVERTIBLE FACTS ABOUT MOTIVATION:

1. You cannot motivate anybody to do anything they do not want to do. Motivation is internal, not external. It comes from within.
2. All people are motivated to do something. Even the person who stays in bed in the morning rather than going to work is more

motivated to sleep. They might be negatively motivated, but they are motivated nevertheless.

3. People do things for their reasons, not anyone else's. The trick is to find out what their reasons are—which you can do by encouraging creative thinking and rewarding all ideas, no matter how silly they might appear—and by asking the "who, what, when, where, why, and how" questions that managers so rarely ask.

The ECR Program was implemented based on Milliken's belief that rewards will encourage innovative thinking among their staff members. ECR was designed to reduce or remove margins for error. The net result of the program is that it has saved Milliken millions of dollars over the years, and not just because they caught a mistake here or found a better way to do something there.

It therefore stands to reason that because this program worked so well for Milliken's internal customers—their employees—then it should apply to the external customer—the end user of the Milliken product. To that end, this imaginative and resourceful company—which battles foreign labor forces that pay their employees pennies per hour—took its idea of "continuing education" to one of their biggest clients: the Chrysler Corporation.

Chrysler buys fabric from Milliken that ultimately becomes the bucket seat cover in their automobiles. That fabric is produced in the form of reams of material that are shaped roughly like a rectangle. That material is ultimately cut and trimmed to become a seat cover in a Chrysler automobile—ultimately shaped like an oval.

GREAT CLIENT FEEDBACK WILL HELP DICTATE GREAT CUSTOMER SERVICE, IF YOU BOTHER TO LISTEN!

Milliken brought Chrysler engineers into their Spartanburg, South Carolina, customer training facility and essentially challenged them to provide their feedback on the product. "Tell us how we can do our job better in order to serve you better," Milliken requested. "We want to teach you how to be a better customer by having you show us how we can produce a more valuable product."

Frankly, no one had ever spoken to Chrysler's buyers this way. This was totally innovative and creative thinking: actually asking the customer what they wanted and then giving it to them.

Chrysler responded by saying, "Okay, Milliken; here you go. If we could get this material from you shaped originally like an oval—the shape that we ultimately cut it to be—then it would save our engineers 19 percent to 21 percent in labor costs."

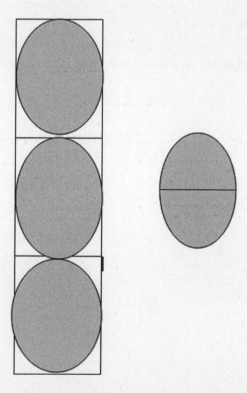

The cost of trimming the product, perforating it, and then producing it into a bucket seat was costing Chrysler a significant amount of time and money. Trimming the product before it left the Milliken plant immediately saved this time and money—thereby making Chrysler a much happier customer. The program was working; all Chrysler had to do was cut the oval in half and produce a bucket seat.

However, this solution left Milliken with an interesting dilemma of their own: What were they going to do with the "floss" in between the teeth of the bucket seat covers? They came up with an innovative and profitable solution: to turn the extra material into rags. Milliken entered a $50 million per year rag industry, simply by listening to the customer. It was a situation in which both the customer and the vendor win.

TAKEAWAY SERVICING AND SELLING TACTICS

1. Work with your customers to come up with creative solutions *together*. Ask them outright how your products could be better or more helpful.
2. Always communicate. Nothing makes an unhappy customer angrier than someone who won't respond to their problem.

CHAPTER 3

FIX THE PROBLEM; DON'T FIX THE BLAME

It costs 5 to 15 times more money to attract a new customer than to keep an existing one.

When I lived in South Carolina, I had to find a new grocery store when my uncles retired and closed our family business—Mack's Cash and Carry grocery. The store I selected shall go unnamed but it appropriately rhymes with the word "ogre." In those days, I would pile my twin sons into my old pickup truck, and we would head into town to grocery shop. We usually bought a minimum of three shopping carts full of groceries so that we only had to make the trip a couple times per month. We didn't shop so much as we swooped, pouncing on dozens of cans of such delectable items as SpaghettiOs, a primary menu item in a house with small kids. Since grocery shopping was right up there with chewing tinfoil for me, it was never a truly enjoyable experience. However, one particular afternoon turned out to be worse than the others.

My sons and I had just run up a $450 tab and were checking out our three shopping carts of groceries. I got home, started unloading, and realized I was missing a six-pack of Diet Pepsi drinks. I called the store that rhymes with "ogre" and got the manager. I explained my dilemma. He placed me "on hold" and disappeared for five minutes while he checked with the irrefutable fountain of knowledge (the bag boy) who testified that he indeed saw "the fat guy" drive out with the six-pack of drinks in the back of his pickup.

STOP THE FRAME

Let's stop the frame for a moment. If I were going to try to rip off "ogre," wouldn't I have gone for the filet steaks? Why pick a $1.79 six-pack of cola? Long story short—the manager came back on and let me know that "The bag boy says you got your drinks, Bub."

"Bub" is a name to which I don't normally answer. "Bubba," perhaps—but never "Bub."

Clearly frustrated with this response, I called his boss the next day and explained my problem. His superior understood those old customer service rules, of which there are only two: (1) The customer is always right. (2) See rule number one. It isn't rocket science.

"Sorry that happened," he explained. "I'll tell the store to give you a six-pack next time you're in."

Now, it just so happened that I was speaking to an "ogre" convention in French Lick, Indiana, the next week. During my speech, I touted the Lexington, South Carolina store's ability to fix my problem and provide quality customer service. It was a terrific war story that I may have even embellished a bit. Knowing that my diet drinks would be awaiting me when I returned the store, I made their company look like heroes.

Two weeks later the check from "ogre" had cleared, and we were in the store, swooping again. This time I'm checking out some $650 of groceries (yes—we eat a lot). I went to my favorite checkout lady— a neighbor of ours—and explained the diet drink situation. "Yeah, I heard about that," she replied. Then she said something that concerned me: "Let me go check with the manager."

The manager came down from on high. (They always hide out in those glass booths with one-way mirrors to see who is stealing candy and such.) His opening statement, in front of six lanes of traffic, was: "Yeah,

I remember you. You're the guy who tried to rip off a six-pack of drinks last time you were in here."

My priest, checking groceries one lane over, looked up at me as if to say, "You didn't bring that up in confession last week!" Obviously, the manager had not gotten the message from his boss about replacing my drinks.

So I suggested that he call his superior and get this straight once and for all. He was screwing up the terrific story that I had told the French Lick group two weeks prior. "I'm not bothering my manager at this hour of the day."

"It's only 5:00 PM," I said. "He's probably not even home yet."

"I'm not bothering him with this nonsense. If you don't like our service, you can shop somewhere else."

Deflated and beaten down, I got home that evening and hit the button on Quicken to see what we had spent on groceries that year. It was over 10 grand—which blew my mind, because it was only August. There were still four and a half more months of grocery shopping (and the months that included "holiday eating," no less.)

THE COST OF LOST OPPORTUNITY

It's been said that every customer you anger costs you 10 to 15 times the amount of money to replace. Losing my business had cost "ogre" over $100,000 because I have never shopped there again—not to mention the fact that I speak a hundred times a year on customer service, and now had a great example of what *not* to do. In fact, I was sharing this story with an audience of newspaper publishers later that year in Orlando when a prominent national journal decided to write it up as a feature column.

The day after the column appeared, I showed up at my office to find six cases of every kind of diet drink that has ever been created sitting on the front steps—along with a note of apology. But it was too little, too late. "Customer service" shouldn't be the oxymoron that this company had made it.

NINETY PERCENT OF CUSTOMERS MAKE DECISIONS BASED ON SERVICE

With every survey today shouting the statistic that 90 percent of customers make their decisions on where to do business based on the service they receive, you had better be paying attention. You have to wonder if the inmates are in charge of the asylum, since companies are spending billions of dollars a year on correcting a problem that should never have occurred to begin with.

Our latest unscientific research suggests that the average amount of money spent on customer service training in the United States today is less than $5 per year per employee, and is nonexistent in many companies. This isn't employees' fault; they simply aren't trained correctly—if at all—and often aren't empowered to fix customer issues. And with more and more business being outsourced to other countries, the problem is only getting worse.

Recently, my brand-new fax machine died. After having to replace ink cartridges on what seemed like a daily basis, it decided one day to simply stop accepting the new cartridges at all. No problem, I thought; I hauled it down to Staples, where I purchased it, and they attempted to install a new cartridge. They got the same results.

The folks at Staples were kind enough to provide me with a toll-free number, which I used to call the fax maker to make good on the warranty I had for the defective equipment. And while it turns out that they were more than willing to replace the machine, I had to jump through an amazing number of hoops to get it done.

Someone who identified himself as Michael answered my first call. He was located in India, which was the first problem. I had to try to reach him at a time that was convenient for him, not me.

Since no one answers their phone anymore—you leave a voice mail and they call you back at their convenience, not yours—I attempted to get in touch during nontraditional business hours (read: middle of the night). However, I'm a trooper. I stuck with it, determined to get a response.

Unfortunately, when I finally got Michael on the phone, I literally could not understand a word he was saying. After asking him to repeat himself several times, we both concluded that he could not solve the problem and the machine was junk. An hour of back and forth led to the decision that he would have the machine replaced—but only under certain rules and conditions.

First, he would send me a voucher that I could use to redeem the cost of a new machine. Secondly, I could not get the machine from Staples, the supplier from whom I had made the original purchase. I had to go through the manufacturer's web site.

In the end, it took the company four days to send me the e-mail voucher. Since they were unwilling to pay for next-day shipping, I was going to be without a machine for another week. I finally gave up, returned to Staples, and bought a new machine—made by the original company's chief competitor.

I will never purchase anything from this major supplier ever again. Yes, they did make good on their defective equipment; but they made the entire process so very unpleasant and difficult that we simply abandoned doing business with them.

Granted, I'm just one guy—a blip on their radar. However, this particular guy speaks to over 100 audiences per year, composed of thousands of attendees. So I'm one guy who becomes many.

When I pointed this out to Michael in India, he was perplexed—and I do not really blame him. Despite the fact that he worked for a major global company, he was not empowered to solve my problem. It was obvious that they had an interest in making their warranty good, but under rules and conditions that I simply could not tolerate. It was easier and cheaper for me to buy a new machine. They have lost my business and will never know it unless poor Michael in India shares my ranting and raving with his superiors.

WHY NOT EMPOWER THE CUSTOMER SERVICE REP?

My question is simple: Since you gave Michael permission to make good on your defective equipment, why didn't you also give him a way to do so without forcing me to jump through a bunch of unnecessary hoops?

All he would have had to do was send me the voucher via e-mail that same day, and allow me to use it at Staples immediately. I would have been a loyal customer for life because I was back in business again.

Instead, they got greedy and forced me to bypass Staples. The folks at Staples were beside themselves. They wanted to simply give me a new machine and replace it with the one the supplier was going to ship. It was not Staples' problem; it was the fax maker's. So I rewarded Staples by buying a better machine at a higher price and I now have a wonderful war story to scream from 100 platforms across the world each year.

THE COST OF MAKING THE CLIENT'S LIFE DIFFICULT

What is the true cost to this company? It is difficult to say. How many other small businesses have suffered similarly—and how many does it take to fix this problem? The fax company was willing to make it good but only on their terms and conditions. A small business like mine cannot function without computers and fax machines. We do not have the luxury of waiting for days or weeks.

What this company *really* lost was the opportunity to ever do business with me and my circle of friends and acquaintances ever again. I call this the cost of "lost opportunity." They had a chance to become a hero in my next book or speech. Instead, they will be the butt of my jokes because they did a very lousy job of doing a very right thing. I don't like having these disappointing stories to tell; I would much rather find heroes and sheroes that I can brag about in my books and from the platform—people who will go beyond the call of duty to make a bad thing good. There are indeed some of those out there—and you have the power to become one.

TAKEAWAY SERVICING AND SELLING TACTICS
1. Fix the problem; don't lay the blame.
2. Good service will pay you huge dividends. Lousy service will cost you dearly.
3. Do the right thing, but do it right. Don't make the customer's life any more difficult.

CHAPTER 4

Always Give Them a Baker's Dozen

Great customer service is about great listening skills.

GEO Prism's Mayday

Back in the mid-eighties, I had the pleasure of doing a series of speeches for a company called New United Motors (NUMMI), a cross between Toyota and Chevrolet. The two companies came together to produce an automobile they called the *Geo Prism*. The most pioneering aspect of this partnership is that Geo was built under a Japanese (Toyota) management system with an American (Chevrolet) workforce. Though this looked on the surface like a potentially ill-fated combination, it actually became the key to their success.

NUMMI did a very novel thing: They gathered salespeople from all over the world into their plant in Freemont, California, and *showed them* how they were going to build this new automobile. In fact, there were so many salespeople that they could not get them all into the building where I was speaking at one time. I had to give the same speech four different times that day to accommodate the sales force.

Throughout the course of the day, I kept hearing some Japanese music ringing out arbitrarily from what sounded like different sections in the plant. At the end of the day, I asked the plant manager what the music represented.

"That was our 'mayday' you heard," he explained. "The music identifies exactly where in the plant we were experiencing a problem. Everyone in that area drops what they are doing and they go and solve the problem."

That is pretty ingenious thinking, I thought to myself, but I had to ask the next question. "What does the union think about that?"

"They thought that was amazing," he exclaimed with pride. "They had never heard of that before!"

New United Motors was another champion that thought differently. Why? Because they were not afraid to throw out the traditional thinking and try something new. The answer is right there in their name: "new" and "united."

BAKER'S DOZEN

These stories are so remarkable because they feature huge global corporations. While some might attest that they're able to think differently because of huge size, that isn't necessarily the case. They just spread the good word faster because they are big. The customer's opinion is what drives this good news—and that's a triumph that a company of *any* size can achieve.

CREATIVE THINKING

One of the most creative thinkers I ever met was my own grandfather, Elias S. Mack, Sr., a Lebanese immigrant who came to this country with a third grade education. Like so many uneducated refugees, he became an entrepreneur by necessity, principally because no one would hire him.

When he arrived on the shores of Ellis Island in New York, he was told he needed to change his birth name, Elias Skaff. "Look, Mack, you need to consider changing your name," said the immigration officer. So, like many other immigrants, he took a new name: Mack.

My grandfather ran a corner grocery store called Mack's Cash and Carry Grocery. Like all small merchants, he built his business on being creative with his customers. "When they come in and buy a dozen apples, you always give them an extra one, because one might not be up to standard. Always give them a 'baker's dozen.' That way, you will never disappoint."

My grandfather was a resourceful man in so many ways. When I was 11 years old, he gave me a book that he claimed would be very valuable to me one day. I opened the book and saw that contained nothing but blank pages. "The book has nothing in it," I observed. "It has no value."

His response was simple: "What you put in it will make it valuable." That book was the first of over 300 journals I now have. At the age of 11, an uneducated immigrant started the process of making me think in a different way. He would say to me, "If you want to be great, you must walk hand-in-hand and side-by-side and in the shadows of people who are great—and greatness will come unto you."

He was telling me that in America, you have choices. "You can be an eagle or a buzzard," he would often say. "The difference is that one bird kills his own lunch and the other picks at the remains. You choose which you want to be."

A JOURNAL FOR THE JOURNEY

My grandfather told me that I needed a journal for the journey. What journey, I wanted to know? The journey called life. He told me that I would want to recall certain moments later in life and that a journal would be the best way to do it.

My first task was to put something in the journal. At only 11 years old, I really did not know a lot about life. "What do you want to be when you grow up?" he asked rhetorically one afternoon when I was visiting him at his home.

I had not given it a lot of thought. All I had ever done in my life was go to school, work in my grandfather's grocery store as a bag boy, play sports like football and baseball, and join the Boy Scouts. My view of life was fairly narrow, to say the least.

However, since I had absolutely no idea, the sky was the limit for me. To be a champion, you have to look beyond the customary boundaries. In fact, you have to remove all borders. That is exactly what my grandfather did with me. He asked me questions like, "What do you think about?" Well, I hadn't given much thought to anything.

But he pushed on. "Where do you get your inspiration?" he asked. "From Sunday Mass," I responded. "Msgr. Joseph Bernadin is a great speaker at Mass." This was the young priest at St. Peter's Catholic Church in Columbia, South Carolina, who gave me my first Holy Communion and ultimately rose in the hierarchy of the Roman Catholic faith to become a Cardinal. "He is a great speaker," I told my grandfather. "I like the way he tells stories."

"Then perhaps you wish to become a priest when you grow up," observed my grandfather. And I actually gave some thought to that process for a number of years until I learned about celibacy. (There went that goal.) However, I think the driving force to ultimately become a professional speaker got its roots from that priest at St. Peter's Catholic Church, who himself was a powerful and yet humble speaker.

My grandfather instructed me to take my journal to church on Sunday and record the things that Father Bernadin said. He taught me to keep a daily account of the events that took place in my life.

My grandfather became deathly ill shortly after he introduced me to my first journal. I recall the summer of 1960 as if it were yesterday. I was only 11 years old, but I helped take care of my dying grandfather. I would fetch him figs off his favorite tree in the backyard or a drink from the kitchen.

I would sit with him as we would watch television together. He hated commercials and insisted that I turn the television off during the commercial break. We would time it and turn it back on two minutes later. Those old television sets took 45 seconds to warm up, so I finally convinced him just to turn down the sound and leave the picture on.

During those television commercials, we would talk about my journal. One of my grandfather's first challenges was for me to make a list of 500 things I wanted to do in my life. I could barely think of 100 things at the age of 11—much less 500. So we would sit with the now-defunct *Columbia Record*—our afternoon daily newspaper—or *The State* newspaper, the morning daily, and the *Lexington Dispatch-News*. We would page through those papers and find articles about different things that we would discuss.

Since I was interested in sports, I naturally put sports-related activities on my list of life goals. Not only did I want to play high school football, I wanted to play college ball and be in the National Football League. Unsurprisingly, I never made it to the NFL, but I probably would not have excelled at high school sports had I not put the pros on the list.

When I wrote down that I wanted to be a priest on my list, it was not the priesthood to which I aspired; it was the thrill of motivating an audience like Msgr. Joseph Bernadin had done so well. His speaking acumen is why I ultimately joined Toastmasters in 1976 and eventually went on to compete in the World Championship of Public Speaking in 1978.

GREAT CUSTOMER SERVICE STARTS WITH EVEN GREATER COMMUNICATION SKILLS

I am one of the few Toastmaster World Champions who made more than one trip to the finals of the competition. I made it all the way to the International Speech Contest in Toronto, Ontario, Canada, in 1977, only to be disqualified for going eight seconds over my allotted time limit. Frustrated at beating myself for going overtime, I went back through the arduous process in 1978 and again made it to the International Speech Contest finals, which were held in Vancouver, British Columbia, Canada, that year. That year, I won the title.

I am fond of telling my audiences today that you have to go through Toronto to get to Vancouver; in other words, you must experience defeat to truly appreciate victory. Champions must think that way. It was not about winning or losing for me; it was about the process of not beating myself. In fact, I rarely speak about the victory in Vancouver these days. I prefer to discuss how I overcame the defeat I suffered in Toronto.

The roots of this entire story were established in the embryo of a journal I had started 17 years earlier in the small town of Lexington, South Carolina, at the encouragement of a Lebanese immigrant who thought it important enough to encourage his grandson to write things down. How blessed was I to have such a mentor in my life!

You Need a Mentor

A mentor will tell you two things:
1. What you are doing right, and
2. What you are doing wrong.

My mentor was my grandfather; he taught me how to set goals in life. For that, I will be forever in his debt.

I recently had the opportunity to review that first journal I wrote, and chuckled at the way my 11-year-old self looked at life. Though I'm amused at the way I tried to spell difficult words, the goals were crystal clear to me. Of the original 500 goals that I wrote down, I have accomplished (or scratched off as "not accomplishable") some 487 of them. No, I'm not going to be a priest, but I would not be a professional speaker today had I not originally written priest on the list.

No, I'm not going to be governor of South Carolina, but I would not have run for the House of Representatives in 1980 if I had not written governor on the original list. I learned that defeat is the process by which we succeed. God knows I have experienced enough defeat in my life, including that race in 1980. I have since found it is cheaper to buy a politician than it is to be one (just kidding).

The goals you establish drive you; they have no borders, no ceilings, and no limits. Today, my list of goals has grown to several thousand, most of which I have accomplished. Though it's been a challenge, it's also been well worth it. This is not to say that there aren't some obstacles along the way; in fact, there are a few major things that make reaching goals especially difficult.

Four Reasons We Don't Achieve Our Goals

1. **We have been *told* about setting goals, but not *sold* on it.** The Bible has an interesting line: "If the eye be single, the whole body is full of light. If the eye be evil, the whole body is

full of darkness." That means to me that if you are focused on accomplishing a goal, your process is immediately improved. You are halfway there. Goals must be challenging, yet accomplishable. They must have deadlines, and you must be accountable to them.

2. **We have not been shown how to set a goal.** If you will simply answer the questions "who, what, when, where, why, and how," you will know how to set a goal for yourself. Answering those questions clarifies the process. It is your road map to success.

3. **We are afraid we are going to fail.** No one likes to fail. It is the single biggest obstacle to setting a goal in life. There's no danger of failing, of course, if we don't even try in the first place.

4. **We are afraid we might** *succeed*. Though it sounds strange, social scientists claim that the greatest reason we do not set goals is because we feel that we don't deserve the success that comes with accomplishing them. In fact, this reason outweighs the rest combined. We truly fear success!

When John F. Kennedy was running for the presidency in 1959, a reporter posed a rather challenging question to him. "Senator Kennedy, if you could be guaranteed to be the next vice president of the United States, would you accept that guarantee as opposed to running for president and possibly losing?" I never will forget Kennedy's response: "Why should I accept number two when number one is available?"

Though Kennedy clearly did not fear success, most other people do. We tend to think we do not deserve it, and accept second best simply because it is available.

What if Kennedy had listened to his peers and taken the vice presidency? He might never have been elected to the top office in the land. How many times have you listened to others' criticism and negative words? My grandfather gave me a wonderful piece of advice prior to his death: "Listen to the criticism of others, but do not support them. There is no such thing as constructive criticism," he explained. "Most criticism is destructive, because more often than not, the person doing the criticizing is criticizing the *performer* and not the *performance*. You have to separate the two."

I was standing in line at my local bank one day behind a young woman who had her little son Henry with her. How did I know his name was Henry? She called him down 15 times while we waited for her to reach the teller cage. "Henry, stay in line." "Henry, get back over here, boy, or I'm going to pop you one." "Henry, you better get right and I mean right now."

She half turned to me and said, "Henry, if you don't straighten up, I'm going to give you to that man!" I did not want him, but I would have taken him after what she said next. "Henry, if you don't straighten up, you're going to end up in jail one day." Would you be surprised to read about little Henry going to jail in 15 years? GIGO: Garbage in and you get garbage out.

OUR TRAINING DICTATES OUR VALUES AND BEHAVIOR

I recall when our twin sons Cory and Jason were in the first grade, the teachers decided to separate them, putting them in different classes. I am convinced they did this because they just did not want to be bothered at figuring out who was who, but we went along with the experiment, which interestingly gave us an opportunity to compare teachers.

Mind you, all teachers have their own style. I won't say one was negative, but she had been weaned on a pickle. The negative teacher would send home the child's assignments: "Dear parent, see that your child does this and this and this. Signed, the teacher."

The positive teacher would write, "Dear pumpkins, this week we're going to work on this task, this task, and this task. It's tough, but you're smart. I've seen your work and I know that you can do this. Signed, With Love, Mrs. Casey."

Which teacher would you rather have? Mrs. Casey, of course!

TAKEAWAY SERVICING AND SELLING TACTICS

1. Always give them a baker's dozen. Promise a lot; deliver more.
2. Great communication skills start with great listening skills.
3. Never fear failure; it is the process by which we succeed.
4. Work with mentors and become a mentor to others. It will make you a better person.

CHAPTER 5

TRUST, ONCE VIOLATED, NEGATES A RELATIONSHIP

If 20 clients are unhappy with your service, 19 won't bother to tell you. Fourteen of the 20 will simply take their business elsewhere.

The late great life insurance guru John Savage was a close friend of mine. His favorite expression was "Trust, once violated, negates a relationship." Was he ever right!

The violation of our client's and customer's trust is the number one thing that causes them to seek products or services elsewhere. Some 19 of 20 unhappy clients won't even bother to tell you—and 14 simply end up doing business elsewhere, probably with your competition.

Take care of your client or someone else will. It is as simple as that.

TAXPAYERS ARE CUSTOMERS, TOO

My weekly column, "Behind the Mike," appears in over 600 publications all over the world. One of our Ohio readers brought to our attention the fact that the local school board canceled high school football and all other extracurricular activities in Grove City, Ohio, just six miles southwest of the capital city of Columbus. Though I guess it's merely a sign of the times, it begs the question: Why? Aren't we taxpayers the clients and customers of government—be it local, state, or national? Why are we summarily dismissed without regard to our thoughts, feelings, or beliefs? Unfortunately, we have to wait until the next election to vote the bums out. They have lost our trust, which is the single most abiding thing they want from us besides our loyalty and our vote.

Normally 11,000 screaming fans should have gathered at Grove City High for something that is a rite of passage for high school kids: a high school football game on a Friday night. It is not just football that was canceled, but a way of life for kids everywhere. Anyone who ever played under the Friday night lights knows that warm glow that comes over you when family, friends, and neighbors gather to cheer on the local kids, win or lose.

Unfortunately, that tradition got the hatchet. Cheerleaders who lead the Friday afternoon pep rallies no longer have anything to cheer about. The marching Greyhound band that normally plays to a capacity house no longer entertains. Sadly, these same financial strains affect school boards in every city and every state.

While no one wants to judge this particular issue, it does raise some interesting questions. It turns out the South-Western City School Board, which includes four high schools, took the unprecedented step of canceling all extracurricular activities after voters failed to pass an operating levy. Now four high schools in Ohio's sixth-largest school district have no sports, no bands, no drama productions, and no student council. Was this a move to get even with the voters?

EVERYBODY WANTS TO GO TO HEAVEN; NOBODY WANTS TO DIE!

Neighbors have turned on one another in anger. I am reminded of the age-old saying: "Everybody wants to go to heaven; nobody wants to die." Everybody wants paved roads and good schools; nobody wants to pay the taxes necessary to pave and build them. Everybody wants quality education for their kids and grandkids; nobody wants to foot the bill.

There is another old saying: "We get the kind of government we deserve." I personally reject that as not exactly being the "whole" truth. The situation in South-Western was extreme but not necessarily unusual. Across the nation, school districts are wrestling with a fundamental question. When money is tight, should taxpayers be funding high school sports? When you put 11,000 people in the stands, one would think that sport should be able to not only pay for itself but all the other sports combined. Unless they are giving away the seats, this should be a no-brainer.

In Mount Vernon, New York, students, parents, coaches, teachers, and community leaders raised nearly $1 million to fund the school district's sports program for the 2008–2009 school year after voters twice declined to pass the district budget and forced the district into austerity mode. The budget was passed—with funding for athletics—for the current school year.

The net result of such extreme measures is that parents will move their kids to other districts that still play football. Let the mass exodus begin—not just of students, but also coaches and teachers. Talk about cutting your nose off to spite your face.

Perhaps the more important question here is: How does one get elected to a school board that looks only to cut instead of looking for solutions? Is this a way of blackmailing a community into a tax increase? If you tried such drastic measures in most small towns, you would have a major rebellion on your hands. The community will begin to wilt and die when you take the blossom off the trees.

Everybody wants to go to heaven; nobody wants to die. This scene could be coming to a community near you.

We Need a Customer Rebellion

Perhaps what is called for is something that the parents in Mount Vernon did to some degree: launch a customer rebellion. When governments do things in a way that angers the populace, they deserve the results of that anger. Unfortunately, you have to wait for the next election to settle the score.

Clients and customers do not have to wait, however; they get to vote immediately. Make no mistake, the people in the affected communities feel just as violated as the client who buys a lemon from a disreputable car dealer.

MAKING LIFE DIFFICULT SEEMS TO BE THE GOAL OF SOME

I was speaking in Hartford, Connecticut, recently when I learned of the death of my uncle, former mayor of Lexington, South Carolina. Naturally, I wanted to get back as soon as possible so that I could make arrangements to attend his funeral in South Carolina and eulogize him.

However, I learned that in order to change my midmorning flight to an earlier one, I would have to pay what amounted to double the cost of the original flight. Fair enough; I understand that airlines are hurting and that fees have to be charged. However, let's examine the dynamics of this.

First, there were empty seats on the earlier flight, which was departing at 6:00 AM, while the more popular, later flight was much fuller. Simply putting me on the earlier flight would have gotten me home in time to attend the funeral without rushing—*and* freed up a seat on the more popular midmorning flight.

I decided not to pay the double air fare—but not without questioning the situation's logic. After all, one would think that the airlines would have been grateful for my gesture of making space available on a later flight by agreeing to get up at 3:00 AM and to the airport by 5:00 AM I asked the gate agent about making the change, but he was operating out of the *Official Airline Customer Irritation Manual*. The airline failed to empower the gate agent to make a heroic gesture that would make a deposit into the all-important "favor bank." That's right; they could have enjoyed positive dedication from a heretofore loyal passenger. They sadly have lost that forever. Mind you, this was not some $50 change fee but double the original airfare.

I actually moved to Orlando, Florida, because I got tired of going there for speaking engagements. I used to fly a lot and have millions of miles with Delta, United, and others, but today, I actually drive to many of my speaking engagements because I live in St. Cloud, Florida.

In the old glory days of Delta, I was awarded a Flying Colonel distinction. I had so many miles with them that any request of this nature was granted and never questioned. Those days are long gone, which is why I moved to Orlando. It is just not worth getting on an airplane anymore. But duty calls and I still have to fly from time to time.

In my mind, I was actually trying to figure out why the fare had doubled. I was still getting the same bag of peanuts and still flying the same distance. What were their real costs of accommodating me in my time of grief? As best I could figure it, the worst that could happen is that I would free up a seat on the later flight that they could actually sell to another poor soul who had to be somewhere that day.

TRUST, ONCE VIOLATED, NEGATES A RELATIONSHIP

The airline lost my faith and trust forever that day, all because of their greed. I am now one of the 20 unhappy clients, 19 of whom will simply take the business to their competitor in the future. They have lost my future business and are totally unaware as to why. They had a chance to gain a lifetime of trust and loyalty with one kind gesture—and instead they poisoned the pool forever.

This same airline brags about its friendliness and the fact that you do not have to pay to check your bags with them.

The fact is they do not want you checking your bags because it adversely affects their on-time departure.

The fact is they have cut so many corners trying to be "on time" that they have made it to the FAA's watch list for safety concerns. Why would they spend millions of dollars advertising their great business practices and then make a bonehead decision like this one?

PROFIT VERSUS PROPHET

This very same airline is the subject of many great atta-boy articles in many customer focus books. Some even call them a "prophet" for the airline industry—but as far as I'm concerned, they're more interested in "profit" than in being a "prophet."

Granted, this is an isolated circumstance, but it does beg the question: What were they thinking? What would have been lost by this—several hundred dollars more "pure profit"? Are greed and profit that important? Wouldn't the airline have a greater perceived value if they had given their gate agent the ability to collaborate with the client for a solution? Was their airfare based on an additional fee for value or just a way to make more money?

Instead of addressing my situation, the airline missed a golden opportunity to address my needs, which were legitimate and timely, not situational or cumulatively punitive to the airline. They never bothered to engage me or diagnose my issues. They never attempted to make any exception to the *Official Airline Customer Irritation Manual*. They were concerned with one thing and one thing only—"profit." They could have been a "prophet" but that opportunity is lost forever.

TAKEAWAY SERVICING AND SELLING TACTICS

1. Take care of your client or someone else will. It is just that simple. If 20 clients are unhappy, 19 won't bother to tell you—and 14 will simply go elsewhere.
2. Build trust with your client, and you earn their undying loyalty and dedication—which is worth its weight in gold.
3. It takes a very forgiving client to come back for second helpings when trust is lost. Most times, they simply won't do it.

CHAPTER 6

SOMEBODY HAS TO
TAKE OUT THE TRASH!

*Up to 90 percent of unhappy clients will
not buy from you again, and they won't
bother to tell you why.*

CLIENT RETENTION SHOULD BE
THE MODEL, NOT THE EXCEPTION

Customer retention is not only a cost-effective and highly profitable strategy; in today's very competitive climate, it is absolutely necessary if you are in business for the long haul. This is critical, given the fact that 80 percent of business comes from 20 percent of your client base.

Still, most marketing and advertising campaigns are so highly focused on attracting new customers that they practically ignore the loyal clients who have been there for years. One of the best examples I can think of comes from the world of the highly competitive wireless telephone industry.

Most companies here have the audacity to offer a huge rebate or free cellular phone to a new customer, while giving current clients the privilege of paying full price. All this does is force loyal clients go elsewhere, which is exactly the opposite of what it is trying to accomplish.

Sadly, one of the most telling statistics of all in the client relations arena is this one: 90 percent of unhappy clients abandon you and they don't even bother to tell you why. They simply fire you as their vendor or provider. Period. No questions asked. No apologies rendered. None expected.

I would far rather have an angry client than one that has no agenda whatsoever. I would rather hear 10 objections to my proposal than one indifferent person who has no opinion. I would rather be slam-dunked by a furious customer than be politely dismissed by one who just doesn't care.

Perhaps *indifference* is the key word in this scenario. To begin with, it is a lot easier to have a discussion with a client than to do so with a prospect. A client has previously made a decision and had a reason to buy from you; a prospect has not.

One of the most powerful aspects about the insurance company I represent, the Knights of Columbus, is the client loyalty that our members offer us. Many of them have as many as 30 or 40 contracts with the Knights, and you can summarize the reason in one word: loyalty. It clearly explains why they purchase so much and are so loyal to us. While I'd like to think that it has something to do with our agents doing a great job in the field, the fact is these people are dedicated to the quality of our products and fraternity.

All I Want Out of Life Is an Unfair Advantage

I have a basic philosophy in life: "All I want out of life is an unfair advantage." The unfair advantage of the Knights of Columbus Insurance is the quality of its people and products. Only two companies in the world have our ratings, a fact that speaks volumes to the 1.8 million members worldwide about who we are and what we represent.

A company earns this kind of dedication over more than a century of providing quality service; it doesn't just "happen." While the persistency in our agency is around 95 percent, it still means that 5 percent of the people changed their minds. By industry standards, 95 percent is excellent. By my standards, 5 percent got away from us—and I want to know why.

Why Do Your Clients Fire You?

Sometimes a client fires you because of domestic or financial reasons. Sometimes they find a better deal or a product you do not offer. You recognize it and live with what you cannot change. However, the things you influence in some way are the ones that should never go unattended.

A client's displeasure with your product or service is an invitation to address a problem. When one of our members calls in to cancel his certificate, my philosophy is simple: "A buying decision is going on, and I want to be a part of it." I don't care whether the commission trail has run out or not. I hate to lose business to another competitor.

If a client gives us profound reasons for switching companies and I do not have a competitive product, I'll be the first to advise him or her to make the move. But more often than not, your competition is preying on your client and simply trying to line their own pockets.

We have a fiduciary responsibility to let the client know when they are making a mistake. Don't let your competition set that table. They are not going to share all the facts. Defend your company's practices, whether or not it's commissionable to you as a salesperson. Doing this screams volumes to your client that their needs are paramount.

Somebody Has to Take Out the Trash

There are occasions when a previous sales representative may have misstated a product or service. In those cases, somebody has to step in and educate that client. Someone has to fix the problem and take out the trash.

The greatest motivational principle in the world is the truth. It's right there in the manufacturer's handbook (the Bible): "And ye shall know the truth, and the truth shall make you free." The truth *always works*—and most of us are not smart enough to be good liars, anyway.

PUT THEM ALL ON COMMISSION

I have always believed in having people on commission, including secretaries and administrative people. My philosophy is simple: Rewarding good behavior begets good behavior. Case in point: While suffering through my four-mile workout on the treadmill at the local sweat factory recently, I was reading a *USA Today* article about the compensation of America's top college football coaches. I have learned two things about compensation systems.

1. If you show me the reward system of any institution, I will show you where they place their values.
2. Second: If you pay peanuts, you generally get monkeys.

What possesses the University of Florida, for example, to pony up $4 million to coach Urban Meyer? Answer: He generates many times that in revenues! The age-old argument from tenured professors about how much more valuable they are to the educational institution than coaches falls on deaf ears for the most part.

The fact is that professors are tenured and coaches are not. You cannot fire a professor, no matter how sorry they are. At least the university can get rid of a coach who's not getting the job done.

Another issue is the range of compensation from one school to another. For instance, the 2009 base salary for Coach Dabo Swinney at Clemson was only $816,850. One could argue that the Tiger IPTAY Club, the fundraising arm of Clemson University, generates as much or more gifting income than the majority of universities and colleges that pay their coaches much higher salaries. Coach Swinney's efforts on the gridiron directly impact the giving—so shouldn't he be on commission? Instead, the compensation for a Clemson head coach was actually reduced by 32 percent when Swinney took over after the previous coach was fired for not winning enough football games.

However, Swinney took less of a hit than Navy head coach Ken Numatalolo. Though his income was reduced 53 percent in 2009, his Midshipmen beat up on Notre Dame for the second year in a row.

Numatalolo's income was a fraction of Charlie Weis's salary, a man whom Notre Dame fired in 2009.

Perhaps they ought to put coaches on commission like salespeople. If you win and generate revenue, you get a piece of the pie. If you win and lose money, you get a smaller piece of the pie. If you lose, you get no pie. That is how it works in my world. I get paid when my feet hit the floor and only after I produce results.

As a matter of fact, I believe you can put almost any job on commission. All you have to do is define what winning behavior looks like and place a value on it. Of course, there are arguments made to the contrary about rewarding people based on performance. What will the union think? What will the rank-and-file think? Will the employees embrace "performance-based" compensation? Will it result in long-range meaningful dollars or just a short-term flash-in-the-pan? And what about the proper mix of compensation elements? Can a balance be struck between short- and long-term incentives, and will it lead to achieving the overall goals of the organization?

Blah, blah, blah. You keep score in athletics—so why not pay for performance? Then when someone cheats, lies, or steals, dock their pay or fire them. How hard is this? Don't reward people who win "at any cost"; reward people who win fairly.

FIX THE PROBLEM, NOT THE BLAME

My dear friend and co-author of another book, Jeff Slutsky, is a marketing guru who founded Streetfighter Marketing, an Ohio-based firm that specializes in unusual approaches to unusual problems.

In our book, *The Toastmasters International Guide to Successful Speaking* (Dearborn Publishing, 1996), Jeff tells many terrific stories about how he made streetfighters out of his clients—one of which comes to mind.

Jeff had a pizza vendor for a client who had to compete with pizza giant Domino's. Domino's vendors used a clever marketing approach that included buying the biggest *Yellow Pages* ad that was available to them through the local phone directory because their research suggested that clients simply called the first ad they could find. Someone who wanted home delivery pizza would grab the phone book and immediately be drawn to the full-page ad on the back cover.

His client was a half a step away from calling it quits when he asked Jeff to solve the problem. Jeff asked his client some simple questions that boiled down to: What is ailing you, and how can I fix it? Answer: The competition is all but putting him out of business. The solution is more business.

Jeff then asked the client how much money he had budgeted to address the problem. He took this figure and said, "Send me half for my retainer and take the other half down to the local radio station that has the biggest audience share in your immediate market area. Buy all the advertising sound bites that you can with that money and use this script: 'Bring us the Domino's Pizza ad from your local phone book and we'll give you two pizzas for the price of one.'"

Within days, the vendor had regained his lost market share and then some. Granted, this was back in the day when people used phone books and pay phones. However, the concept of bringing a competitor's coupons to match or beat the price is a valuable one in most industries. Huge grocery chains are constantly advertising that they will honor or in some cases double the rebates offered by others. In this dog-eat-dog competitive world, you have to use the "unfair advantage."

TAKEAWAY SERVICING AND SELLING TACTICS

1. Remember, it's the client who fires you. Sadly, 90 percent of them won't even bother to tell you why.
2. Somebody has to take out the trash. You can fire the person who caused the problem later. Just make the client whole again now!
3. Client retention is markedly cheaper than the cost of finding a new client.
4. All I—and most people—want out of life is an unfair advantage.

CHAPTER 7

YOU ARE NOT THE ENEMY BUT PART OF THE SOLUTION

Ninety-six percent of unhappy clients do not complain of poor service.

Every bit of research on the issue suggests a number of alarming facts about the customers who don't bother to complain about getting lousy service. Alarmingly, 96 percent of unhappy clients do not complain. A closer look at this fact suggests three understandable reasons:

1. It's not worth their time.
2. You aren't listening.
3. You won't respond.

If you gather around your brain-trusts and posed these comments to them, it would come back smelling like this: "You'll do okay if you just handle the complaint." As we are fond of saying in our insurance agency: "Somebody has to take out the trash."

If a customer goes to the trouble to complain but remains unhappy, they will be even *less* loyal than the one who doesn't bother to complain in the first place. A big part of the problem is that most businesses have very lousy complaint processes. You have to jump through far too many hoops to get from point A to point B, and most customers decide that it's simply not worth their time. This immediately discourages them from ever doing business with you again—even if you were to drastically cut prices. Customers rarely care about price; they always care about the level of service you render. In the end, the company's response, or lack thereof, tends to be the real problem. Why is that?

MR./MS. CLIENT . . . YOU ARE A LIAR AND A THIEF!

Many so-called customer service reps launch the complaint process with the belief that the customer has a hidden agenda; that is, they are simply looking for something for nothing. Why not go ahead and just flat-out call your client a liar and a thief?

Moreover, these "fixers" rarely fix anything. In fact, they compound the problem by running the poor customer through the drill: "Did you follow the detailed instructions? This damage could not possibly have happened on our end; did you do something to cause it?" In the end, the poor customer throws their hands up in the air and walks away, never to do business with you again.

Does that mean there aren't people out there who are looking for a handout? Absolutely not. Scam artists, liars, and cheats exist. The key is to use your skills to find out what the real issues are. Learn the power of asking open-ended, rhetorical questions that begin with the words "who, what, when, where, why, or how." These questions lead to open-ended responses.

THE PERSON ASKING THE QUESTIONS IN THE INTERVIEW PROCESS CONTROLS THE INTERVIEW

When an inbound call comes to your phone, don't ask the client, "How can I be of help to you?" if you really don't want to be of help. It insults their intelligence. They are already angry that the gadget or service they purchased does not work. Why compound the problem? Acknowledge it.

THERE ARE FOUR KEYS TO DEALING WITH THE COMPLAINT:
1. Soften the complaint.
2. Isolate it; don't ramble into other areas. Work on the problem at hand.
3. Rephrase it to the client so that both you and the client are clear on what the actual issue is.
4. Work together toward a solution.

LET THEM KNOW THAT YOU ARE NOT THE ENEMY

Some time ago I was on a flight to Maui for a conference. I had to connect through O'Hare Airport—a zoo on a good day, but almost unbearable during the cold, harsh Chicago winters. On this particular day, it was snowing and sleeting harder by the minute. Flights were being delayed and canceled because of the weather.

The gate agent was trying her best to get as many people transferred to a plane that had be de-iced and was about to depart for Hawaii. I'm in line behind a belligerent man who was using the "bigger hammer" approach to try to get his way. You know the type. "If I hit her with a bigger hammer I'll get my way."

You could tell how perturbed the agent was. Finally, she quietly leaned across the counter and in a soft voice she said: "Sir, there are two people in the world who give a damn about your problem . . . and one of them is fast losing interest."

Finally, the confrontational passenger understood that the likelihood of him getting on that plane lay squarely in the attendant's hands—and so he straightened up. Ultimately, she got him on board. She knew the important lesson that you sometimes have to give an aggressive client a "time-out" if they insist on being unreasonable. When a client complains, it is perfectly okay to let them know that you are not the enemy and that you are seriously interested in solving their problem.

MAKING A MOUNTAIN OUT OF A MOLEHILL

Another common problem with complaining consumers is that they often want to magnify the problem beyond its true scope. We all have rules that we have to live by; they exist for everyone's benefit. Keep the complaint within the rules. You can't perform miracles and you can't fulfill unreasonable expectations simply because a client has been harmed. You can't give a client a $2,000 computer because his $100 fax machine failed. Make them whole—not "whole times 20."

It really requires getting the mountain down to the molehill. Isolate the problem, and then solve it aggressively. If the client's interpretation of a solution is different than yours, either you are not being fair or they are being unreasonable.

Some of the latest television ads have the cook stripping the deluxe hamburger of lettuce, tomato, and onion because the customer ordered a value meal. While the intent is to have some humor in their message, little things like charging for a refill of iced tea and running the tab up for a pickle make the entire experience just plain irritating. The solution is to clearly define the rules.

THE IRRITATION FACTOR

Clearly, grumpy people don't need to be heading up your client relations department. You have to have polite, courteous people handling this arena—because for most of these customers, you are already too late.

For instance, client requests to surrender a policy with the Knights of Columbus typically travel by snail mail to our home office—which easily could take a week, based on where clients live. By the time it arrives and gets funneled down via e-mail, another day or two might be lost. Once received, we try to pass it along to the responsible agent that same day. However, the agent may chase the client by phone for several days before he can secure an appointment to help him with his request.

In other words, by the time the agent gets in front of the member, a couple of weeks or more have passed—and the client is clearly irritated.

He was thinking he'd have his check the next day, and is upset that the process took so long. The reason for the delay, unfortunately, was that the client went around the agent directly to the home office—a big "nuisance factor" for the customer. Fortunately, our agents are trained to handle these issues in a diplomatic fashion. Remember, it's much more difficult to converse with a prospect who has fired you than it is with a client who has retained you.

MINIMIZING DELAYS . . . FEEL, FELT, FOUND

The name of the game is to *minimize delays*. Get the word out quickly to the people responsible for the situation. In this digital age, that shouldn't be too difficult a task. It is critical to maintain a sense of urgency when dealing with an unhappy client. A great opening statement follows the "feel-felt-found" formula: "Mr. Client, I think I know how you feel. I have felt that way also when trying to get a problem corrected. I've found that the best thing to do is to get down to the business of correcting it. Let's get to the bottom of this. . . ."

Now you are right in the middle of the problem-solving effort and clearly on the client's side. Show a sense of urgency and respect; that's usually what they want most.

TRAIN THE CLIENT ON HOW TO BE A BETTER CLIENT

One way to educate your clients on how to be better buyers of your products and services is to let them know the most effective way to address an issue at the time of the sale. Ask them to be specific and brief in the expression of their issues. Make 800 numbers and e-mail addresses available so that people have a quick way to express their annoyance with the situation. Inform them about your company's processes, so that you can deliver the best possible results to them as quickly as possible. If a problem is ongoing, ask the client to retain letters, e-mails, and phone calls so that it is easier to reconstruct the history and thus work toward a suitable solution.

Let's face it, there are going to be problems. Customers today have been conditioned and understand that things occasionally go wrong. They simply want viable solutions.

HERE ARE 10 TIPS TO ESTABLISHING AN EFFECTIVE EDUCATION PROCESS:

1. Provide all contact numbers, e-mail addresses, and other communication vehicles at the point of sale so that the client is aware of how to get issues resolved.

2. Stress the importance of names, addresses, and contact information so that the proper people can reach them to resolve their issues.

3. Let clients know how you can best serve their needs when an issue arises.

4. Explain the process thoroughly; if possible, provide them with sample letters of common problems that surface.

5. Emphasize how critical it is to provide specific dates, places, amounts, and other details when communicating their message to you.

6. Let the client know that irrelevant details will only slow their request, and that they should focus on what needs to be fixed.

7. Find out what their favorite communication method is, and use that to get in touch with them. Many people want to call an 800 number, and others only want to do business digitally. Give them all the available options, and let them decide.

8. Create an easy follow-up process to make sure the issues were resolved.

9. Avoid being wishy-washy with them. Get to the point of how the issue can and will be resolved.

10. Be firm on agreed deadlines and deliver what you promise based on facts, not emotions.

TAKEAWAY SERVICING AND SELLING TACTICS

1. Ninety-six percent of unhappy customers will not bother to complain. They will simply take their business elsewhere.

2. Not everyone is out to get "something for nothing."

3. Make mountains into molehills by isolating and defining the problem.

4. You are not the enemy. You are part of the solution.

5. Ask good open-ended questions to get to the root of the problem.

6. Educate the client on what good customer behavior looks like.

7. Become clients' ally and proponent.

8. Act quickly on all issues. Follow up to make sure things were handled correctly.

9. Be thankful for those who do complain. It means that you have a client you can retain.

CHAPTER 8

COMMUNICATION SKILLS MEAN EVERYTHING; JOIN TOASTMASTERS OR DALE CARNEGIE

In many service industries, the quality of service is one of the few variables that can distinguish a business from its competition.

In most industries, people have a multitude of choices. With the proliferation of the Internet, those choices have been multiplied many times over. The only thing that remains distinguishable between you and your competition is the service you render.

Service is literally five times—some experts even claim 10 times—more important than any other single factor. If the quality of your service is the discernible characteristic that sets you apart, wouldn't it make sense to focus more on this than on anything else?

A major part of this problem is poor communication skills that so many possess today. Even if your product or service is terrific, it will be negatively impacted by an inability to effectively communicate its use to the client.

Clients want to do business with people they genuinely like, and being "likable" is enhanced considerably by your verbal skills. Unfortunately, there are precious few courses in the educational world whose focus is enhancing verbal communication skills. The good news is there are two very tried and proven vehicles in the commercial marketplace that are available to the public: Dale Carnegie and Toastmasters.

Dale Carnegie courses began in 1912 and have spiraled across 75 countries throughout the world. They focus on what they've deemed the five drivers of success:

1. Build Greater Self-Confidence
2. Strengthen People Skills
3. Enhance Communication Skills
4. Develop Leadership Skills
5. Reduce Stress and Improve Your Attitude

Toastmasters International's roots were first planted in 1912 as well, when Ralph Smedley formed the very first club in Santa Ana, California. This nonprofit entity's mission statement is to promote communication, public speaking, and leadership skills. Toastmasters has served over 4 million people and currently has some 250,000 members in 108 countries in the Toastmasters International speaking world—all of whom are part of some 12,500 clubs worldwide.

I first joined Toastmasters in 1976 when an insurance client of mine invited me to a breakfast club meeting in Cayce, South Carolina. I have been a member since and attend meetings almost every Friday morning at 7:30 AM in Kissimmee, Florida, near my offices. I continue to hone my own communication skills with this excellent forum. So many people have trouble speaking on their feet. In fact, a London newspaper once published a survey that concluded that standing on your feet and giving a speech was the most difficult thing that most people would ever have to do. In fact, it was listed as the chief fear among all things considered by the respondents.

There must be many reasons for this. However, we have found—in the hundreds of seminars that we have done on public speaking—that the principal reason most people are afraid to speak in public derives from one thing: an absence of knowledge.

WHAT'S IN IT FOR ME?

Most speakers don't take the time to ask themselves the basic question that their audiences are asking: "What's in it for me?" So they ramble aimlessly in six different directions with no thought as to their presentation's goal or purpose. Regardless of the forum, you should approach each situation with similar ammunition in your arsenal. Whether it's a point-of-sale PowerPoint to sell new business, an attempt to conserve clients who are about to walk out the door to your competition, or a presentation you're giving to thousands, the fundamentals are the same.

THE BASIC STRUCTURE OF ANY SPEECH INCLUDES THREE KEY COMPONENTS:

1. Knowing *what* you want to say.
2. Knowing *how* to say it.
3. Having something to say about it *yourself*. That is, you should not be simply repeating what someone else has said about a subject.

Effective communicators must remember that above all else, they are in the idea business. When you run out of ideas, you're out of business. You're no different from the grocer or car dealer; when you're out of inventory, you close your shop.

Speaking is much the same way, whether it's to a convention or to your local Rotary Club. That audience is saying eight words . . . I want, I want, I want, I want! Give them what they want by studying your audience before you commit the first thought to paper.

THE SIX PS

There's no secret to excellence in public speaking. It's fairly simple: Know what to say about your subject. Your job on the platform is to inspire action in the uninformed. You must wake people up, and that takes what we call the "6 Ps"—*Proper Preparation Prevents Pitifully Poor Performance!*

BEFORE YOUR NEXT PRESENTATION, ASK YOURSELF THESE SIX QUESTIONS:
1. Are my opinions respected?
2. Do I possess a basic philosophy?
3. How do I develop my philosophy?
4. Do I understand the reason for success and failure?
5. What do I expect?
6. Will it have staying power?

How does one overcome fear? There are several ways to answer that question, but the best answer is a three-word quickie—practice, practice, practice! When I won the World Championship of Public Speaking for Toastmasters International in 1978 in Vancouver, British Columbia, I was interviewed by the Associated Press, and they asked the key to my victory. My response: I practiced the winning speech over 300 times—in the car, in the shower, on a jog, and in my dreams.

SPEAK WITH CONVICTION

Practice isn't the only key, however. The speaker must be able to release his or her convictions, faith, and knowledge about the subject. You have to be sincere and genuine in order to be persuasive. And remember, there's no substitute for product knowledge.

One way to overcome fear is to address areas about which you know a great deal. Personal experience is the best subject matter, so use other people's experiences, illustrations, and the "vignette system" of constructing speech. This is a series of stories tied together to key in to a basic theme.

You might also use the system of speaking in acrostics. For instance, your presentation to a sales and marketing group might be built around the acrostic S-U-C-C-E-S-S. Confidence on the platform comes from knowing your subject matter, and you can stay on track with an acrostic.

(It also gives your audience a hint when you're going to be through, if you're bombing!)

You must be confident without being cocky. One of the biggest problems with most speakers is that they lack humility. You must be impeccable in your appearance, both physically and mentally. We advise our clients always to dress for the occasion. For a man, in most cases, this is a three- or two-piece suit with a white shirt and a tie. Black, grey, or brown colors are acceptable in most circles. For a woman, never dress flashily. It is far better to be conservative than liberal in color and manner. Dress as you would for an important board meeting.

THE K-I-S-S FORMULA

Though this sounds like an elementary piece of advice, it works. Use the K-I-S-S formula: Keep It Short and Sweet! Simplicity is perhaps the most appreciated—yet least understood—virtue in a speaker. Reduce both the size and the number of words you intend to use. Don't ramble in your speech. Get to the point. Important things must be said, not read. Use some humor in your presentation, but don't try to be a stand-up comedian. This is a very dangerous area and can bring instant disaster to a presentation if not handled properly. Try to keep things light, and above all, don't take yourself too seriously. No presentation should be without some lighthearted humor.

So you know what you want to say; you know how you'd like to say it. What comes next? You should be constructing your speech just like anything else: It must have a solid foundation—in other words a strong opening. You can and will lose your audience in the first five minutes if you don't immediately grasp their attention.

Your next phase should be the body or the content of the speech—the most critical part. Work from an outline and build the body of your speech around it. CPAE Hall of Fame Speaker Paul Harvey, who earned high fees for a speech, used humor in some form every seven minutes in his presentation. Make your closing powerful and conclusive. Many speakers open a speech with a quote and close it with the same quote, tying the theme around the quotation.

Remember, there are three components to a successful presentation: the speaker, the speech, and, most importantly, the audience. A successful presentation requires that all three come together organically. No matter how great a speaker you might be, if your topic is presented poorly, it will bomb. If an audience doesn't have any interest in the material, it will crash—no matter how great a speech and speaker may be! Always be aware of these three key ingredients.

TIMING

Your timing is a tricky part of delivering your speech. Again, the K-I-S-S formula is the best. Unless you are delivering a seminar, keep your points minimal. Use only your own material in your outline the first time around; after you've completed it, then add your research. Build in your support materials and your quotes after you have constructed the basic pattern of the speech.

Before writing the final draft of your speech (and I do sincerely believe you should write it out word-for-word), test yourself on a tape recorder. If the presentation isn't polished, try to hone in on why. Test the basic ideas out. Are they logical? Are they in order? Do you have trouble following the theme? If *you* do, then your audience surely will, too.

One mistake that a lot of speakers make is failing to put enough of themselves in the speech. Don't let this happen to you. People will pay attention to you if they feel that it is "you" making the speech. Personal stories and anecdotes bring you great credibility.

DELIVERY IS CRITICAL

How important is your delivery? In the thousands of speeches and seminars I have done over the past four decades, this has always ranked as the most important area of concern for our seminar participants. A few tips to consider:

1. Dress impeccably.
2. Never drink beforehand.
3. Don't eat either if there's a chance it will make you uncomfortable.

Always acknowledge the host or master of ceremonies in your opening. Try to ensure favorable speaking conditions such as an adequate microphone and good lighting beforehand. Test your voice early to make sure everyone can hear you. Always arrive early and test the microphone and lights.

Tweak your presentation's gestures to the audience size and occasion. If you are in a large room with over 100 people, you may wish to gesture outside the perimeter of your body. A smaller room would dictate that you should confine your gestures from your waist up, from your sides in, and not above your shoulders. Additionally, your body language should portray a positive physical manner. Moving around disarms your audience and allows you to become more intimate with them. You should always try to have as much eye contact as possible. If it causes you to lose your train of thought, look just over the heads of your audience. In most cases, they'll think you're looking at the person directly behind them.

Voice inflection and proper modulation are also critical. One way to improve this aspect of speaking is to record every presentation you make. You want to hear what you did right as well as what you did wrong.

DRAMATIZE THE STORY

Subscribe to what I like to call the 80/20 rule for speaking: 80 percent of your success on the platform is directly related to your enthusiasm, and 20 percent is directly related to what you said. Humanize and personalize your subject, then dramatize the story with proper timing and good word pictures that lead the audience along a path that should closely parallel your outline.

Visualize your speech; don't force your material. Be honest, sincere, and open with your audience. Make them partner with you in your speech. After all, they are pulling for you to succeed.

Finally, don't ever abuse the clock. Start and stop on time. There's nothing ruder to the audience and others involved in a program than a long-winded speaker who takes more than his allotted time.

Use your closing to provide some inspirational material that will cause your audience to want to take action. Short poems, quotes, stories, or vignettes are perfect for a strong closing. Remember the "three S formula"—stand up, speak up, and shut up.

Cat got your tongue? Not if you practice what you preach!

TAKEAWAY SERVICING AND SELLING TACTICS

1. Join Toastmasters immediately. The best way to improve your client service skills is to improve your communication ability. Confidence comes from knowing that you know how to communicate.

2. Consider taking a Dale Carnegie course to improve your human relations and memory skills. Carnegie offers excellent training.

CHAPTER 9

PROPHET VERSUS PROFIT . . . WHY NOT BOTH?

Providing high-quality service can save your business money. The same things that contribute to customer happiness also lead to increased employee productivity.

The quality of the service you render is one of the few variables that will distinguish you from your competition. True enough, but it's the consumer who defines the quality of that service, not you.

In today's "What-have-you-done-for-me-lately?" corporate world, many businesses are more interested in the bottom line than they are the line they feed their customers in their so-called mission statement regarding the quality of the service they say they are committed to render. The cuff doesn't match the collar. Their actions don't match their promises.

They profess to be prophets of good service and yet they are more interested in profit than in their prophecy. Make no mistake; one must be profitable to stay in business. However, ethics and values must be part of the process. Providing high-quality service can not only save your business money, but it can also make you more profitable.

One of the most interesting by-products of a happy customer base is that the people who work with you, for you, and around you in your organization serving those same customers are also happier. The entire organization profits from this prophecy.

Can an organization be profitable and still be ethical? Perhaps the more important question might be "How can an organization be profitable without being ethical?" Ethics aren't an option; they are a requirement.

PROPHET VERSUS PROFIT

In my adopted hometown of St. Cloud, Florida, my local Catholic church embarked on a project called the St. Thomas Aquinas Medical Clinic. Our mission is to provide free medical care to the uninsured and underserved in our community. The project operates under the umbrella of the Diocese of Orlando's 501(c)(3) tax-exempt status.

Scores of doctors and nurses willingly and freely offer their time, talent, and treasure to provide for the medical needs of the underserved in our community. The dynamics of this project have never ceased to amaze me.

Here you have this group of unselfish medical professionals who put in a full day of work at the hospital or office and then they come to the clinic after hours to assist those who can't get help elsewhere.

Being inquisitive about such things, I questioned one of the doctors about why he was doing this. His answer was candidly simple. "This is the one place where I can practice medicine without regard to cost or to the time it takes to do the job correctly."

What if every business approached the customer in the same fashion? The clinic's founder, the late Dr. Romualdo Dator, established the roots of this clinic in the very definition of the word *service*.

I had known Dr. Dator for years and yet we seldom had the opportunity to spend time with one another. Both he and I were so busy in our respective work lives, we seldom had time for anything but family.

It's interesting that while we lived in the same town for so many years, I didn't really get to know the man until I recently got involved with the clinic in a fundraising capacity.

As much as anyone, Dr. Dator was responsible for the resounding success of the clinic. My respect and admiration for his commitment to the clinic is matched only by the hard work he put into convincing dozens of doctors and scores of nurses and lay volunteers to donate their time, talent, and treasure to making the clinic the success that it is today.

The people involved in the St. Thomas Aquinas Medical Clinic are all hardworking folks who willingly give of themselves for others. The service they render is free and unconditional.

Wouldn't it be nice if all businesses could approach their business in a similar fashion without regard to the bottom line?

Wouldn't it be nice if magnificent customer service could be rendered unconditionally?

Free medical clinics are not a novel idea, but the very basis of these ventures offers up a unique matrix around which one could build any successful business. Start with the highest quality of people you could want in any business. Quality here could be defined as someone who loves what they do so much that they would do it for free, and in fact do.

Just because they are not paid for their efforts does not mean these folks are not vetted thoroughly. In fact, the background checks required to provide them with the sovereign immunity that allows them to practice medicine without fear of liability are more thorough than those offered in private practice.

In other words, not only do they show up and work for free but they are beaten up pretty thoroughly to gain permission to "give their time freely and without charge." If your heart is not in the right place, you simply would not do this.

By example, a venture like a free medical clinic has its very roots in old-fashioned customer service. One of my favorite movies is *Doc Hollywood,* starring Michael J. Fox as Dr. Benjamin Stone and Julie Warner as Vialula, better known as "Lou."

Everyone likes this flick because it reminds them of the little hometown they came from years ago. My birthplace of Lexington, South Carolina, was much the same. All these communities had one doctor who delivered most of the town's offspring.

Ours was the late Dr. James S. Liverman. He brought me, all of my 10 brothers and sisters, and dozens of our cousins into this world along with most of the other children of that era in Lexington County. The vast majority of them were delivered in the tiny Liverman Clinic on Church Street in Lexington, usually with little fanfare but great efficiency.

Dr. Liverman and his lovely wife and nurse, Katherine, took care of the many medical needs of thousands of Lexington residents over several decades in my hometown. Like Dr. Aurelius Hogue, played by Barnard Hughes in the movie *Doc Hollywood*, Dr. Liverman knew his patients intimately. Hogue treated one youngster who got into his daddy's chewing tobacco with a Coke. In their day, doctors practiced medicine in the patient's homes, not in an office. They could better evaluate a patient if they could see how the patient lived.

Every small town has a character for mayor. In *Doc Hollywood*, David Ogden Stiers plays the part of Mayor Nick Nicholson, dressing as a huge squash for the annual squash festival hosted in the town. Our mayoral characters were Eli Mack Sr. and Eli Mack Jr., my grandfather and uncle, respectively, both of whom served Lexington as mayor.

I fondly recall my grandfather grilling out behind his home, cursing in Arabic when my grandmother Tina got the flames too high for the neighborhood shish kabob. Like Mayor Nick Nicholson in the movie, Jiddo (Arabic for grandfather) had to step in and offer advice to lower the flames before putting food on the grill. My fondest remembrance as a youth was watching Jiddo grill for the Lexington High football team after another huge Wildcat victory.

Dr. Liverman was as much a part of the success of Lexington's athletic programs as anyone who ever played or coached there; some would probably say more so. On February 18, 1984, I spearheaded a banquet to honor Coaches J.W. Ingram and E.T. "Charge" Driggers.

Over a thousand people came to pay homage to the coaches that night. When Coach Ingram rose to thank the gathering, one of the people he credited for Lexington's success on the athletic fields was Dr. James S. Liverman.

"In all the years he served as our team physician, he never rendered a single bill for any medical attention he gave to our players," remarked Ingram. "He accepted whatever the insurance paid. He never once charged us for any team physicals and rarely did he ever miss a game at home or away."

Nowadays, you can't even get most doctors to return your phone call, and forget about one coming to your home to render medical attention. This is not a slam on current doctoring; it's just a simple fact.

I suspect the vast majority of folks who Dr. Liverman saw over the years never had any insurance. I know my parents never did. Doctor Liverman would simply tell my mother and father, "Send me *what* you can *when* you can." He never once dunned them for a penny and God knows with 11 kids needing medical attention, he rendered plenty over the years.

My guess is that he was owed hundreds of thousands of dollars by the time he went on to his greater reward.

I recently received a sweet note from Katherine Liverman thanking me for my columns over the years, citing the many memories I fondly bring up on a weekly basis. Those memories are borne out of the kindness and love of people like Dr. and Mrs. James S. Liverman.

There's no need to thank me. We should be thanking you, not just for all you did for the community over the years, but for providing all of us with fond recollections of the way we were in a kinder, gentler time in our lives.

Prophet versus profit? What kind of customer service representative are you?

TAKEAWAY SERVICING AND SELLING TACTICS

1. Do you love what you do so much that you would do it for free?
2. Do you go into every relationship with your client thinking about what is in their best interest, not yours?

CHAPTER 10

PERCEPTION IS REALITY

The first 30 seconds of a call or meeting set the tone for the remainder of the contact. The last 30 seconds are critical to establishing lasting rapport.

What kind of first impression do you think you give? Would you do business with you based on your initial appearance and impression? Perception is reality, and the client's reality comes from a first impression—be it good, bad, or indifferent.

When my three sons were growing up, we had an incentive plan in place in our home that offered ways for them to earn money on a daily basis. We never believed in giving allowances. We charged our children to live in our home—a fee they could offset by earning money to do certain tasks.

We also required our sons to invest the money they earned. If their checking account exceeded $500, they had to transfer the money into an investment of some sort. They were allowed to choose, but they had to invest it. If they failed to invest it, I forewarned them that I would confiscate it. One of my twin sons—who was 11 at the time—looked up *confiscate* in the dictionary and declared he would not allow that to happen. Fair enough, I told him. How do you want to invest your money? He thought on it for a day or so and came back to me.

"Dad, I'd like to buy some stock!" I asked him where he learned about stock and he advised me that he had been reading my *Wall Street Journal* and watching CNN. Well, that one threw me for a loop; *I* don't even read my *Wall Street Journal*.

Surprised and impressed, I asked him what kind of stock he was interested in purchasing. Without a moment's hesitation, he told me: Wal-Mart. I was stunned because at that particular point in time, Wal-Mart was taking off like a rocket. Again, I had to ask the question: "Why Wal-Mart?" His answer was so simple and revealing. "Two reasons, Dad. Number one, the toy department is always well stocked. Number two, the parking lot is always full."

Is perception reality? You bet it is. Is your toy department well stocked? Is your parking lot full? Are you equipped with the product knowledge to assist your clients in their time of need? Are you empowered to provide solutions to your client's needs? Knowledge has a short shelf life and requires updating. It's a facet of doing business that you and your colleagues must continually fine-tune.

LISTEN TO THE CRITICISM OF OTHERS, BUT DON'T SUPPORT THEM

My grandfather Elias S. Mack Sr. was one of my mentors growing up. I remember him sharing his philosophy with me. "Hiyetti, find out what the poor people are doing, then don't do it." I asked, "What do you mean by that, Jiddo?"

"Find out what the successful people are doing then emulate their good habits."

I recall one afternoon during the last summer of my granddaddy's life, he said to me: "Hyetti, listen to the criticism of others, but don't support them." I asked, "What do you mean by that, Jiddo?"

TAKEAWAY SERVICING AND SELLING TACTICS

1. Perception is reality. Is your toy department well stocked? Is your parking lot full? Do you have the knowledge to assist your client in their time of need?

2. Is your character perceived correctly or do your clients misjudge you based on your initial impression?

3. If the client's first impression is not what you want it to be, do you repair the damage to make their last impression the one you want them to have?

CHAPTER 11

BE A HERO OR "SHERO" . . . FIX THE PROBLEM . . . AND THEN FIRE WHOMEVER CAUSED IT!

Ninety-five percent of unhappy clients will become loyal clients again if their complaints are handled well and quickly. Don't fix the blame; fix the problem!

THE MINIMUM SHAFT JOB

Unhappy clients will become loyal clients again if their problems are simply handled well and quickly. I believe today's customers are conditioned to what I like to refer to as the *minimum shaft* theory; that is, what's the minimum hit I'm going to take today? They expect stuff to go wrong and hardly give it a second thought. They have complete confidence in Murphy's Law: that whatever can go wrong, will. I like O'Toole's Law better. He said Murphy was an optimist.

People are almost stunned when planes leave on time and baggage actually arrives at the airport of destination. They don't know how to act.

Moreover, they believe that "planned obsolescence" is very much a part of life in general.

Some time back I was traveling through the Atlanta airport, as was the custom for me in those days. Every flight out of South Carolina, when I lived there, connected through Atlanta or Charlotte. Since Delta Air Lines was my most frequent carrier, I got to know all the folks at Hartsfield Airport on a first-name basis. Many actually thought I lived in Atlanta.

One day I was connecting through Atlanta and I needed some orange juice to mix in with some medication I had to take to lower my cholesterol. I'm about to miss my flight so I'm rocking back and forth on two feet trying to push the line along. When I finally got to the front of the line, I proceeded to order a glass of orange juice with no ice. The powered medication that I had to mix with the juice simply would not mix with ice.

Ignoring my request completely, the vendor proceeded to pack the cup full of ice and flavor it with some orange juice. In my more polite days, I would have simply fished the ice out of the cup, poured in my medication, stirred it, and been on my way. But this particular day was not a great day for me, so I decided that I would ask again for a cup of orange juice with no ice. "Sir," I said politely, "I ordered the orange juice without ice."

This time he actually heard me, but instead of starting over and pouring me a new cup of orange juice, he proceeds to put his fingers over the cup's edge and strains the OJ through his fat fingers into a second cup. He didn't even bother to fill up the second cup. He simply slapped the lid on it and shoved it back in front of me as if I didn't see a thing.

There was a time when I would have simply walked away and would not have paid for the juice, but too much crap like this had already happened on this particular day and this was the straw that broke the camel's back. I took the lid of the cup and threw it at this idiot and told him, "You got your fingers all over it—so I figure you should go ahead . . . and wear the rest of it!" Then I walked off.

I think we go through our lives as customers saying what's the minimum shaft I'm going to get from some idiot today? We're conditioned not to even bother to expect good behavior from the outset because so few people provide it.

People automatically go into relationships expecting the worst, and anything short of that disaster is considered a "moral" victory. Sadly, this is the general public's most common mentality; let's-cut-our-losses-and-move-on is the defeated consumer's mantra.

CUSTOMER BEING PROACTIVE

As a customer seeking better performance from those who serve me, I have found it more convenient to be proactive in this process. I've decided that if the folks whose job it is to take care of my problem aren't any good at it, then perhaps I can encourage them to get better; train them, if you will.

I also figure that if I can thank God for a meal before I sit down, perhaps I should do the same thing for the people who serve me in some capacity. I actually learned this from my wife, Christine, who is the champion thank-you note queen of the world. All you have to do is remotely attempt to accomplish something on her behalf and she'll write a note to everyone from the CEO on down. She never met a customer service survey she didn't like.

I, on the other hand, feel like I'm paying for service and I shouldn't have to thank people for doing their jobs. Still, I've learned from Christine that honey/vinegar concept of writing thank you notes.

THANK-YOU NOTES PAY HUGE DIVIDENDS

When I lived in South Carolina, I used to hear horror stories from my colleagues about their bad experiences in airports. I thought to myself, if they'd just stay loyal to one airline, they'll reward you back. After all, it was working for me. I am not saying my planes have never been late, or that luggage does not occasionally get lost. On balance, though, most of my flying experiences have been very good over the years.

I learned early on that the best way to get good service on any airline is to simply expect it—and let people know that you're expecting it as well. The first thing I do when I get on an airplane is I ask the flight attendant for the name and the address of their supervisor.

"Is there some problem?" they always ask. "No, there is no problem. I just want to write them a thank-you note for the wonderful service I am about to receive."

Don't laugh; I swear to you, it works. I found that one of the criteria the airlines use for promotion of their people is the number of complimentary letters they have in their files. Conversely, complaint letters can be a killer for promotions. I always keep blank cards in my carry-on luggage with my picture and biographical sketch on one side, and room to write a note on the other. I use these to write a sincere and honest thank-you note to the flight attendant's supervisor, praising him or her for the wonderful service I received during my flight. I specifically mention the flight number, the name and ID number of the flight attendant, and the explicit action that he or she took to make the flight more enjoyable. I am always honest and detailed. And since I never seem to have a stamp with me, I usually ask the flight attendant if they will pass it on to their supervisor.

As everyone deplanes, you hear "good-bye, good-bye, good-bye, good-bye. . . . Oh, good-bye, Mr. Aun! It was so wonderful having you on board today. And won't you please fly with us again."

Over the years, I have flown Delta Air Lines so much that I was writing to a guy named John Hume in Atlanta twice a week. He was the director of the flight attendants for Delta at Hartsfield International Airport. I wrote so often to him that we got to the point where we shared Christmas cards each year. He got so many of my letters that he recommended me as a speaker for Delta.

He always politely responded to every "atta-boy" or "atta-girl" that I would send to his people. One day, I got a personal letter from Mr. Hume. "Dear Mr. Aun: Stop writing. I retired last year!"

Thank-You Notes Contain Four Simple Ingredients

A thank-you note is one of the most important things you can do for anyone. It contains four simple ingredients.

1. **Do it quickly**. A note written six months after the fact is an insult.
2. **Keep it short**. It doesn't have to be a dissertation.
3. **Be specific**. Let the person know "why" you are taking the trouble to thank them; tell them exactly what they did that made the experience so pleasant for you.
4. **Write it personally**. A handwritten note always works much better than something formal or electronic.

If thank-you notes work so well to get customer service representatives to actually do their jobs, imagine how stunned you would feel if a client representative actually took the time to write you a note in return. In all my nearly 40 years in business, I can count on one hand the number of thank-you notes I received from people with whom I did business over the years. I simply do not understand this behavior. Your mother taught you better!

In our insurance agency, we teach a four-tier thank-you note system. When you first secure an appointment for an initial interview, you send them a thank-you note that not only reminds them of the appointment, but suggests what you wish to accomplish during the interview.

The second note goes out to the client upon the completion of the first interview. It can be written in advance and placed in the client's file. Once the appointment concludes, add a handwritten P.S. at the bottom of your generic note and drop it in the mail the same day.

The third note thanks them for having done business with you and summarizes what you are going to accomplish on their behalf when you initiate the application for their insurance coverage.

The final note is written thanking them for having the confidence to do business with you and your company. More important, it sets the stage for your next interview with the client and paves the road for the next sale. It should also ask for referrals to other family members or friends. The deeper you go with a client, the more business they will refer to you.

Many of our clients have as many as 20 and 30 life insurance, long-term care, and annuity contracts with us. We are constantly horizontally marketing to find new clients, but make no mistake; we want to assist each client we already have to our maximum ability.

Learn to thank others for the good works they do. It will pay you huge dividends.

Takeaway Servicing and Selling Tactics

1. Clients want you to fix the problem, not the blame. You can fire who caused it later. Be the "hero" or "shero" who solves the problem.
2. Thank you notes are the most powerful and least expensive marketing tool available to anyone. Use it or lose it—the business, that is!

CHAPTER 12

NOTHING TAKES THE PLACE OF GOOD MANNERS

The customer defines good service and a good sale is GOOD SERVICE.

Make no mistake: The customer's expectations are clearly driven by the promise you made at the relationship's outset. More often than not, people simply want what they bargained for.

So put yourself in your client's shoes. Ask yourself what you would expect if you were them. I would hope that the customer service representative on the other end of the line would have a smile in their voice. And the best way to do this is to put a smile on your *face*. We train our insurance agents to keep a mirror on their desk and make sure that they're smiling before dialing the phone.

Another key to acting professional is to literally look professional. My wife used to kid me when I would get up on a Saturday morning and go into my office to make phone calls to set insurance appointments for the following week. I actually put a tie on to get into the proper frame of mind. Okay, so I'm a little obsessive compulsive; however, I guarantee that you'll be perceived as a professional if you act professionally. If that means "putting on your uniform" to get into the game, then suit up! Whatever it takes to motivate one into action may be different for another.

When you're only half-committed, this fact will come through the telephone to your clients. The age-old mantra in a Dale Carnegie course I took years ago still rings in my ear: "Act enthusiastic and you'll be enthusiastic!" When you show up "casually" for the gig, the perception is "easy-come-easy-go." Casualness leads to casualties. Take the process seriously and you'll be treated seriously.

Your clients are constantly evaluating you throughout your conversation. If you constantly interrupt them, you'll simply be furthering their anger and frustration. Remember, the client is the one who defines good service, so let them define it. Shut up and listen. Let them vent, and use the opportunity to take good notes while they are expressing their thoughts. Make sure to ask permission before doing so if you're meeting face-to-face. It's one of the highest compliments you can pay your client. You are, in effect, saying to them: "What you're saying to me is so important that I want to write it down."

Ask them to expand on that which you do not understand. Don't be afraid to get clarification from a client who has an issue. Try to find out what it will take to make them "whole" again, but be very careful not to make promises that you are not empowered to fulfill. Remember, it's not about getting them *everything* they want; it's about trying to find a win-win solution.

Years ago, I was a member of the Lexington, South Carolina, Rotary Club, and learned a great deal in my brief tenure there. My fondest memory of the time spent in Rotary was their four-way promise.

1. Is it the truth?
2. Is it fair to all concerned?
3. Will it build good will and better relationships?
4. Will it be beneficial to all concerned?

Those are great principles to apply to any relationship with *any* client, because they are solution-driven. Still, even the best of intentions is sometimes sidetracked by unavoidable delays that frustrate and anger a customer. In principle, the Rotary promise sounds wonderful. In reality, what's "fair" to one might not be construed as fair and equitable to another.

This demands that you maintain good manners as you try to forge the gap that often exists between the client's expectations and your capability to deliver on those expectations. Do it with a smile and as much tender, loving care as possible. There will be times when a solution cannot be reached, when the client deserves to have their money refunded to the extent of the law. But it's always fair to ask, "What was the problem?" Seek a solution short of giving away your products for free, but do it with dignity and manners.

FIRE THE CLIENT

In the 1993 movie *A Bronx Tale*, actor Chazz Palminteri, who plays Sonny, advises his young protégé, Calogero—known simply as "C"—to write off the $20 that was owed to him by a neighborhood kid he had befriended. "You get to rid him from your life, and it only cost you $20." Sometimes it's better to take the loss and move on—because you can never make some people whole no matter how hard you try. When that happens, it's okay to fire the client.

Yes, I do remember telling you that the client defines good service. However, their definition isn't always the *correct* definition. The customer isn't always right—despite all the colloquialisms that suggest otherwise—but they *are* always the customer. Find a way to help them be right by doing "right" by them.

My grandfather learned early on the importance of cultivating the customer and defining excellence in the customer's mind when he first opened his business. His sons continued to run a profitable grocery store for decades after he passed on. Their success was largely driven by a desire to always please the customer. If you were having a bad day, you simply dropped by Mack's Cash and Carry and the Mack boys would go to work on you, cheering you up.

In addition to having the very best beef in Lexington, South Carolina, they offered some of the best advice to thousands of consumers who ventured into the friendly confines of their little grocery store. They always had a warm greeting for anyone who walked through the door, asking you repeatedly how you were and always doing it with a sincere smile. Every man was "pal."

As early as I can remember, I worked in his grocery store bagging groceries. As I grew older, I took on other roles and was allowed to pedal groceries on the store bike to his many local customers around the town of Lexington.

In those days, we delivered. Though the store's name included "Cash and Carry," it could have easily been called "Mack's Credit and Delivery" because nearly every customer who came into the store at one time or another "put it on the tab." Times were tough and many people, especially teachers and county workers, were paid only once a month—so my uncles had to carry them until the end of the month. They never charged a nickel's interest on that money—another token of good faith to the community of Lexington.

TAKEAWAY SERVICING AND SELLING TACTICS

1. Is it the truth?
2. Is it fair to all concerned?
3. Will it build good will and better relationships?
4. Will it be beneficial to all concerned?
5. Act enthusiastic and you'll be enthusiastic!
6. Fire the client.
7. Shut up and listen.

CHAPTER 13

CLIENT LOYALTY IS
EARNED, NOT GIVEN

*It's the client's loyalty to you and
your institution that multiplies business.
Good service leads to increased sales.*

Customer loyalty has its roots in the basic premise that you must assume that the customer is telling the truth. Even though it may occasionally appear that customers lie to manipulate a situation, you still have to give them the benefit of the doubt—because the consequence is losing their loyalty to a competitor.

When you focus on making a customer instead of making a sale, the needs of the consumer come first. The so-called golden rule suggests that we should treat others as we want to be treated.

However, I don't *want* most people treating me the way they treat themselves. Instead, I think we need to treat customers the way *they* want to be treated. That's how you build loyalty.

LOYALTY IS A DERIVATIVE OF ETHICS

Loyalty has its ancestry in ethics, which is simply based on doing the right thing. For nearly four decades, I have been an insurance agent for the Knights of Columbus Insurance. Our entire premise for doing business is based on the loyalty of our 1.8 million members to our superior insurance program.

It's no accident that the Knights of Columbus is extremely committed to doing the right thing for its members. Someone once asked me if you could be profitable in business today and still be ethical. How can you be profitable *without* being ethical, I wondered? When your values as an organization and a company are clear, the decision to do the right thing comes easily.

Loyalty is not earned with discounts or prizes. Loyalty is earned over the course of time with solid, consistent service and quality products. For nearly four decades, I have watched the Knights of Columbus insurance say "NO" to get-rich-quick products and schemes that would put the organization and its clients in harm's way. Those decisions came easily because their values were so crystal clear. For that reason, many of their members have literally dozens of contracts with the company.

Marketing requires that you increase awareness both horizontally and vertically. While you must always be looking for new people to see and sell, this won't do you any good if you're "one-and-done" with those clients. Customers have choices; they will go elsewhere. This is what makes customer loyalty so critical in today's highly competitive sales environment.

The Knights of Columbus sells insurance only to its members, their wives, and dependent children. If you're not a member, you're ineligible for their products. This highly focused environment ensures loyalty to and from the institution. The company is constantly bringing in new members through its "horizontal" marketing efforts. Once they are in the fold, the goal is to keep the client base as happy as possible.

LOYALTY IS A TWO-WAY STREET

I eat at the same restaurant every morning; I've done so for over a decade. Why? In addition to getting treated like royalty by the good folks down at my local Village Inn in St. Cloud, Florida, I have a special deal with them.

I live about five minutes from the restaurant. Before I leave my home, I phone them and order what they have come to refer to as a "Mike Special." A "Mike Special" is a scrambled egg, sliced tomatoes, and nothing else. They must have "caller identification" because no matter who takes the call, they simply say "I'll put your special in." We never really even have a conversation.

When I arrive at the restaurant, I make my way to my usual table where the eggs and sliced tomatoes are waiting. Other restaurant patrons freak out a little bit. I get this look: *How does he rate?* I quietly hand my waitress my gift card that they debit for $5.00 — $3.16 of which is for the meal and the balance for the tip. When I'm done, I quietly get up and walk out. Many of these same people don't know that I've already paid for the meal; some actually think I skipped out. In fact, one of St. Cloud's finest followed me out of the restaurant one day and asked if I had paid my bill. The policeman and I had to go back in and get the matter cleared up. He actually thought I was trying to score a free meal!

My devotion to Village Inn and their kindness to me has been the subject of a number of articles that I have written over the years in my syndicated weekly column. People from as far away as Vancouver, Canada, have actually come to the St. Cloud Village Inn when they visit nearby Disney World because of an article they read.

You may think this is a trivial example, but it truly shows that loyalty is a two-way street. I would bet that your clients want to have that same type of intimate relationship with you, whether you're selling life insurance or eggs and sliced tomatoes.

TRUST, EARNED OVER YEARS, CAN BE DESTROYED IN SECONDS

Plato said that "Only a man who is just can be loyal, and that loyalty is a condition of genuine philosophy." You earn intimacy whether it's in a marriage or a relationship with a client. Though once violated, trust may damage a relationship, trust is also what often brings customers back. Trust gives you the benefit of the doubt. When you unintentionally or intentionally mislead someone, they are less concerned about the lie that you told and more concerned about whether they can ever believe you again in the future.

This, of course, is why customers simply take their business elsewhere. They change vendors, and frequently, you have no idea that you have lost them. This is the most frustrating thing of all for most companies—to lose business without even knowing it. I would far rather have a livid customer than one who simply disappears silently. If you know you have a problem, then you can address it.

The customer is most vulnerable when they trust you. Client intimacy isn't about blindly jumping off a bridge with a client; it's about being down below to catch them when they make a bad decision. Clients want to trust you; they are tormented when you let them down, because it negates their decision. The most common reply from these unhappy clients is: "We trusted them and this was our reward." Once violated, all intimacy in a relationship is lost; rarely do clients forgive.

Trust is about the mutual confidence your client and you have in one another. It is founded on the clarity of purpose you establish with your client and doing what you say you're going to do. It, in fact, is a pledge of honesty to your client and yourself.

HAPPY CLIENTS WANT INTIMACY IN THEIR RELATIONSHIP

It is clear that clients want an intimate relationship with the people with whom they choose to do business. Every study reinforces that basic premise. It exists in every institution, be it the home, in church, in business, and even in the military. No matter the environment, loyalty and trust are not garnered in a day but rather are earned day-by-day. Conversely, blind loyalty to any institution can lead to catastrophic failure.

Abraham Lincoln said, "If you once forfeit the confidence of your fellow citizens, you can never regain their respect and esteem. It is true that you may fool all of the people some of the time; you can even fool some of the people all of the time; but you can't fool all of the people all of the time."

TAKEAWAY SERVICING AND SELLING TACTICS

1. Trust, once violated, negates a relationship.
2. Customer loyalty is earned; it is not a given.
3. Loyalty is a two-way street. Both you and the customer benefit.

CHAPTER 14

NIBBLE AWAY AT CUSTOMER SOLUTIONS

It's the customer's motivation to buy, not your need to sell. Motivated customers not only buy more, they are loyal and committed.

IT STARTS WITH ASKING GREAT QUESTIONS

We need to find out what's on the client's mind—and that starts with asking great questions. These are the open-ended questions we've previously discussed that require a detailed response: "who, what, when, where, why, and how" questions are absolutely critical to success.

Avoid questions that start with "Did, Would, Could, Should, Can, Do, and May" because they will elicit a yes/no response, and you want your client to expound on what's bugging them. If you lead with these words, then be prepared to have a follow-up question to draw them out. These will prompt the client to vent their concerns. It's a lot like paddling a canoe upstream; if you don't keep paddling, you'll go backward. You have to work through situations, and the person asking the questions is the one who's controlling the interview. When clients start posing questions, it's your job to respond with nonthreatening, information-gathering questions. That's the only way to find out the client's motivation.

But what happens when an irate client literally lambasts you with a complaint and then refuses to give you an opportunity to respond? How do you deal with it? In simple terms: Don't let the client overwhelm you. Reinforce that you are not the client's enemy and that you want to help. However, if you're not allowed to engage the disapproving customer, it's hard to solve their problem. Sometimes you have to fire the irate customer until they can at least give you the space you need to ask questions and help resolve their issues.

Sometimes, the more irate a customer is, the more likely it is that they will make unreasonable demands that you can't possibly fulfill. Try to come to the conclusion as to what will make them whole again. There are several ways to deal with this kind of an unmanageable customer:

1. Diagnose the issue.
2. Get the client to define what *they* think might be a solution.
3. Be prepared to make an offer that will make them whole again.
4. Don't promise more than you are prepared to deliver.

This can occasionally become a negotiation ploy in which the customer is expecting far more than you can deliver—or than they deserve. You can't throw in a free computer because a printer is not functioning. The client has to be reasonable and you have to show fairness.

How do you say no to an unreasonable request? You must approach it in a well-mannered way. After all, nobody likes to hear "no," and it's even more frustrating when it is fueled by emotion. You must adhere to the company's policies but honor your responsibility to the customer as well. Approach the circumstance with balance.

Some problems just can't be solved on the spot. What if you don't have the widget that the client is asking about in stock? The client is quick to ask, "Why don't you have it? You're supposed to be in the business of selling widgets? I don't understand!"

The answer in this case is to step up and admit it. "Mr. Client, we clearly dropped the ball on this one. We've always tried to be here for you in the past, but there has been a run on widgets this week. May I express ship you the widget as soon as we get it? Does that sound good?"

FAIR ENOUGH?

The sweetest words in the English language are "Fair enough?" They don't provoke confrontation, but rather suggest compromise. They are soothing, transitional words that invite a solution.

When a client raises questions about what you did or did not tell them, this can become a battle of he said/she said. Poorly trained marketing people are generally the source of these problems, when they promise more than they can possibly deliver. Now the client has completely lost trust in your company, and their motivation is severely hindered by this disappointment.

You must reply immediately and positively, using the feel-felt-found approach. "Mr. Client, we did not hold up our end of this relationship, and I know how you probably feel. I've felt this way myself when I was disappointed with the service I was expecting from a company. It's my job to make every effort to repair this and regain your trust. I will personally oversee this entire process—fair enough?"

Avoid trying to defend the indefensible; there's no need to try to defuse a bomb that has already gone off. This is both a waste of your time and an insult to the client, and it demonstrates further indefensible behavior. The client perceives it as a cover-up. If your butt is already showing, it's a little late to try to cover it up—so own up and move on.

How do you deal with the unannounced price increase? Let's face it, the cost of a widget may vary, and increases are sometimes going to happen. Don't try to explain away that which may not be justifiable to begin with. Perhaps they previously bought the widget on sale, and that accounts for the increase. Perhaps oil prices zoomed last week, and the cost of shipping the widget skyrocketed accordingly.

Whatever the circumstances, in the customer's mind, they are taking the hit. You can't put the toothpaste back in the tube but you can try to find out why there is such a disparity in the price. If it's possible to do without angering the customer further, ask them if you can take a look in their files for the receipt or record of the previous order. Introduce it in the following way: "Here's what I can do for you. We will credit your account for the difference on this increase. However, please be aware that future increases may occur from time to time. We always want to remain competitive, but costs do go up from time to time. Fair enough?"

What happens when the client demands a full refund on the item? Suddenly the debate has shifted to price and price alone. One simple solution: If the item can be returned, give them their money back and save the customer's future business potential.

There are even car companies nowadays that allow buyers several months to return the car if they don't like it. Though this may invite "buyer's remorse" and encourage people to return the car, you must stand by that kind of promise if you make it. There's only one way to handle this: GIVE THE CUSTOMER THE REFUND!

One way to examine your customer's motivation is to revisit their reasons for buying the widget in the first place. Having this information handy can be incredibly helpful when handling a complaint. If you know you cannot make a full refund for the widget, then you can offer a compromise. This is a fair approach to all parties, especially if the widget has some age on it. Beware of the precedent you are setting, however, since you may be encouraging this customer's next return.

You might hear a protest along the lines of "You guys did it last time I was here! Why can't you do it again?" Let them know that this kind of compromise is a one-time offer of goodwill and should not be interpreted as an open opportunity to take advantage.

The insurance company I represent had a client who complained he was not made aware of the tax consequence of surrendering his life insurance policy. Since the policy had enjoyed major gains over the years, he got hit with a tax bill. While it was not our responsibility to pay his tax penalty for him, the client did make a good argument that we should have forewarned him of the consequence of surrendering the policy. Since there was no way to prove whether he was aware of the problem, we made a one-time offer of "goodwill" on a compromise.

The good news is it brought our attention to the matter and we've now changed our policy to ensure that all clients are made aware of these consequences. While this is perceived by some as a favor, the fact is it is not our job to do favors; it is our job to fix problems. We believed that we dropped the ball and should have put the client on notice of the tax penalty—and for that reason, we struck a compromise.

If you tell people you're going to do something, then *do it*. If you tell them you're going to call them, then do it. If you tell them you're going to fix something, then do it. Don't make promises on which you cannot deliver. This is further fuel for the fire that is already burning out of control.

IT'S NOT SURGERY THAT KILLS; IT'S DELAYED SURGERY

This is a favorite saying of mine. What it means: More often than not, when you address a problem early on, it won't fester into an unsolvable dilemma. Address the problem before it becomes a catastrophe. Taking ownership of it provides you with great credibility and helps to regain the customer's trust. You can do this by first acknowledging the client's profound disappointment in the way things went down. Set aside the emotion by recognizing it, and then deal with the facts. Formulate an action plan in the structure of a statement on which you and the client can agree. Confirm the terms and ask for acceptance. Put it in writing so that you won't experience the proverbial "nibble" that some clients resort to in order to get some extra piece of pie. If you agree on terms of a deal, stick to the agreement.

TAKEAWAY SERVICING AND SELLING TACTICS
1. Understand what the client's motivation to buy really is.
2. Put the emotions aside and deal with the facts.
3. Don't nibble away at the solutions. Ask open-ended, "WHO, WHAT, WHEN, WHERE, WHY, and HOW" questions.
4. Admit when you're wrong, and focus on fixing the problem. The earlier you do it, the better off both you and your client will be.

CHAPTER 15

You Can Only Be Responsible for One-Half of a Relationship—Yours!

Customers do business with people they like. Be nice; it pays.

There's no question about it; folks would rather do business with people they like, and they will go out of their way to avoid people they don't like, regardless of price. Some of this goes to the very issue of how we network with one another.

A good question to pose: Is my net *working*? When I do business with people, am I more interested in what's in it for me or what I can bring to the relationship with the client? An obvious and misplaced focus on ourselves is one reason why clients fire us.

When all things are relatively equal, people want to do business with people with whom they already have a relationship. That's the nature of today's highly competitive business environment. The answer is clearly found in one word that we've already discussed at length: TRUST. Likability, perhaps more than ever, is the great equalizer in relationships. Even if you have the best price or the best terms, it may have less influence on the client's decision to do business than the rapport that you've established.

Your likability can be defined in so many ways but the common ground that people share is the very essence of what networking is all about. Are you confident that you give off good vibrations to the folks with whom you do business? Try putting a smile on your face; that's step number one.

Social science research suggests that people judge one another based on nine basic components:

1. SKIN COLOR

Now, there isn't much you can do about the color of your skin. It's naïve to think that people do not judge the book by the cover, and equally naïve to think that prejudice no longer exists today. It does, and it isn't limited to racial preference. It has everything to do with what the client believes—so deal with it accordingly. I used to weigh over 300 pounds, and I know for a fact that I had clients who held that against me. I had a bariatric bypass in 2002 and lost over 130 pounds—and I know as well that people saw me differently after I had *lost* the weight. Some people make judgments based on appearance; the more prepared you are to deal with this, the better.

2. GENDER

I must admit that I prefer dealing with a female salesperson over her male counterpart—and I don't think I'm alone in feeling this way. Perhaps it's due to what I honestly feel is a greater sense of empathy that women appear to offer. Perhaps it is because I perceive them to be more patient and understanding. Whatever the reasons, I personally prefer dealing with a woman. The bottom line, of course, is that there is little you can do about your gender. You *can* affect the amount of patience and empathy you show to customers—so work on what you can control.

3. AGE

Like your skin color and your gender, there is little you can do about your age. People's preferences in terms of age vary; but they tend to want what they want, be it younger or more mature.

I've found that there is genuine age bias in the speaking business. Having been working in it since 1974, I have learned the hard way that my younger colleagues are often picking up engagements that were my domain for many years. Many of the folks in their audiences are younger and therefore the perception is that the speaker should be closer to their age. To that end, many of my colleagues have changed their marketing accordingly to adjust to older markets. A lot of industries face this challenge, and everyone has to adapt to overcome it one way or another.

4. APPEARANCE

The first three items on this list, by and large, are done deals. You can't do much about them, alas; but you can do *a lot* about your appearance. The old six "Ps" acronym comes to mind: Proper Preparation Prevents Pitifully Poor Performance.

In the insurance business, as in many face-to-face professions, you have to be thoroughly prepared for every interview — and that means looking like a professional. On two occasions in my nearly 40-year career, I have witnessed agents showing up at appointments looking like slobs. It is simply unacceptable to show up in a golf shirt or to be tying your tie on the way up to the front door.

While there are countless books out there on how to dress for your role, the main thing to remember is that *neatness counts* — and it isn't difficult to achieve! You can have tailor-made shirts and $200 ties, but all your credibility goes out the door if they have coffee stains on them. I always suggest that our agents carry a spare shirt and tie with them at all times. Consider it your own insurance policy. If you haven't spilled something on yourself yet, be patient; it's just a matter of time. Be prepared.

No matter what you do for a living, people make a note of your appearance. And while being impeccably dressed doesn't necessarily guarantee sales, being sloppy can lose them in a heartbeat.

You don't get privileges based on seniority, either; just because you've been around awhile, you don't get permission to be careless. I'm similarly bothered by the notion of "casual Fridays." If you're going to take off mentally and in the way you dress, why not just take the day off rather than showing up and slacking off?

As a speaker, we always counsel our peers in the business to dress at the level or slightly above the level of your audience. Even if you don't deal with your clients on a face-to-face basis, the way you dress says as much about your self-esteem as it does about the respect you show for your clients. It's a known fact that people respond positively to your physical appearance. Again, it might not always make the difference in whether you close the sale, but it can definitely cause you to lose one.

In the speaking business, our clients make decisions in today's world on having witnessed a speaker or having watched their video feed. I have always contended that meeting planners and bureaus aren't looking to choose a speaker, but rather are trying to determine which ones they *don't* want. They are not selecting; they are eliminating.

Clients have choices in every arena today. Why give them a reason to eliminate you—especially one that's 100 percent in your control?

Rule of thumb: Dress for inclusion. Dress at least on the same level as or a notch above your client. Avoid styles that stand out or call attention. Men need to go with safe colors that won't cause them to get scratched. While women have more leeway, they too have to avoid extremes.

Dress in a way that allows you to dress down. For our agents in Florida, always be prepared with your coat in the car and wear it into a business situation. But if you're visiting with mom and pop across a kitchen table, a coat might be overbearing and a shirt and tie would be sufficient. Your appearance can make or break your relationship with your client. Take it seriously.

5. FACIAL EXPRESSIONS

Facial expressions can be powerfully positive, or they can be deadly. They can cause you to lose business instantly, whether you are in a face-to-face interview or even over the phone. Even people with whom you're speaking on the phone can hear the "smile" (or frown) in your voice.

Nonverbal communications transcend into very specific interpretations made by your client. This tendency dates back to our ancestors and our evolution. Animal species display certain facial expressions that are developed in primates. While human species advanced in terms of verbal communication, we still depend largely on nonverbal cues to sell our message.

Emotion tends to show in most people's facial expressions. When you're angry about something, it's hard to put a big happy smile on your face. Yet failure to do so might cause you to lose your client. Remember this philosophy: "Be wrong so that others may be right." Realize that unlike the first three things on the list, we can do something about our facial expressions; after all, it's part of category four (your appearance). Since you can control your half of this relationship, do so. Just be nice, smile, and never underestimate the power of silence. Often it isn't what you say that closes a deal; it's what you *don't* say.

Sadly, I remember my very first sale of a home to a client when I had just entered the real estate business. My closing line sounded like this: "Are you sure you want to do this?" This client ended up buying—not because of me, but in spite of me. I'm not very proud of that but the client told me later that I was young (19) and stupid, so he gave me the benefit of the doubt and bought the home anyway. Not all clients will be that forgiving. However, when I asked him why he bought from me in spite of this blunder on my part, he simply stated that "Your facial expression showed honesty, integrity, and concern for my well-being. That was good enough for me."

6. Eye Contact

Eye contact is one of those things that can hurt you if you do not use it correctly. You literally can intimidate people if you stare them down. Clients who maintain eye contact may be inviting you to give them more information.

In certain cultures, eye contact is not only intimidating—
it is considered rude. However, in North America, people who
fail to make eye contact are usually interpreted as being untrust-
worthy. In other cultures, it is considered impolite or aggressive—
an implication of hierarchy and aggressiveness and thus considered
rude. Other cultures invite it. Your job is to be a good listener and
interpret the circumstances.

You can give people space and still maintain eye contact—
usually a sign of respect and genuine interest. An open mind starts
with open response on the part of your client. When you look
someone in the eye, you are saying to them nonverbally, "What
you are saying to me is important!" However, when someone
looks away from you, you tend to lose that sense of intimacy and
elicit disengagement. Be careful when determining that the person
in deep thought about an issue is disengaged; they may be simply
sorting out the facts in their mind.

7. BODY LANGUAGE

This is a more critical area for anyone doing business face-to-face
with their clients, but don't think that because you are speaking to
someone over the phone that your body language doesn't display
itself vis-à-vis your voice and your comments. It does. Many tele-
marketers, for example, actually stand when addressing their clients
as if they were speaking to them face-to-face. Surprised? Don't be.
It works. You must remain in the mood of the moment.

Body language is even more critical when you are in face-to-
face situations. Clients take their cue from the evidence your body
language emits. When clients read your nonverbal cues, they process this information through the prejudices of their own mind and
make subconscious conclusions about your credibility and whether
they want to proceed with their relationship with you. So does
your body language show positive persuasion; or are you being
pushy and overbearing?

A variety of studies have indicated that 7 percent of our influence comes from the words we say, 38 percent comes from our

tone of voice, and 55 percent comes from our body language. Conclusion: More than half of your influence is clearly communicated through your body language, your posture, and the signals you emit. Consider the fact that aggressive or dominant body language may make clients feel threatened, whereas attentiveness might invite real interest on their part. Your clients may respond with body language that also speaks volumes about their interest in you.

For instance, their eyes may roam if they are bored. They might tend to look at anything or anyone but you. Some may fix their eyes on an object to avoid eye contact. Bored people will involuntarily show other signs such as tapping their toes, drumming their fingers, or bouncing their feet, all of which shows a genuine lack of interest.

Closed body language would suggest many of these same things as well. When clients' arms cross tightly and legs cross firmly, they are saying, "I'm not letting you in." Tension increases because you may be coming on in a confrontational way and this is their defense. Crossed ankles and the figure-four (ankle on opposite knee) are additional signs further exacerbated by looking away or attempts to change the subject.

Conversely, open body language invites engagement. Arms are open, and the client leans forward. They are essentially inviting you into their world and are eager to hear what you have to say. This relaxed behavior doesn't necessarily connote a buying signal, but it suggests that they are open to your offer.

When there is body tension, we tend to clench our fists or fold our arms tightly to suppress our frustration and anger. It's almost involuntary. When our client's palms are open and held up, they may be pleading for our help and involuntarily saying they only want to not be hurt. When people show power in body language, it is a sign of many things—from respect to confidence. Touching another person is a power symbol and can be threatening.

Whatever your client's methods are, mirror them yourself. Watch them closely and they'll proffer a hint. They will give you the clues, but you must be aware.

8. PERSONAL SPACE

There is an undefined region that most people have around them that they regard as psychologically *theirs*. Invasion of that personal space often leads to anger and discomfort. This anxiety creates victims—and victims don't buy anything from anybody.

The "undefined region" is classified very differently across cultures. Though there is no clearly designated space requirement, most people will respond immediately if you invade their personal space by backing away, folding their arms, or showing other signs of defense.

There are a variety of reasons people don't want you standing too close to them. We all have our boundaries, some of which are better defined than others. The important thing is to discern your customer's comfort level and act accordingly.

9. SENSE OF TOUCH

The final area that clearly affects how others judge you is your sense of touch. Like the topic of personal space, one must proceed with caution here. You can *touch* people without *touching* people, by stirring their hearts and minds. Great marketers know the value of providing their clients with good information on which good decisions can be reached. People can make good decisions if they are provided with quality information. Therefore, our job as their salespeople is to light the path, clear the way, and help clients avoid the potholes that may come with incorrect decisions. That's all about touching their head with good information.

When they stray from the path with a wrong decision, we must then touch their hearts and help them to get back on track. After all, it's a lot easier to help a client than it is to help a prospect. Valued relationships are built on trust and maintained with trust. When you touch their hearts, you also touch their minds.

TAKEAWAY SERVICING AND SELLING TACTICS

1. Socrates said, "Know thyself." We need to understand our own strengths and weaknesses.
2. Know that you can control two-thirds of the things that people use to judge you. If you want an unfair advantage, study the list and take control of those things you can change.

CHAPTER 16

LEAD THE CLIENT
TO SOLUTIONS

*You will receive the greatest value
by remembering "The Three Ls," which
are very simple, and critical to your success:
Listening, Learning, and Leading.*

Some customer service representatives are so good at what they do that disgruntled clients actually leave feeling very *positive* about the experience. One has to wonder exactly how they manage to do this.

Before she passed away, my marketing representative, Kathy Gunter, was easily the most talented client relations representative I had ever met. When studying the traits that made Kathy so great at her job, I couldn't help but notice that she developed her client relationships like no one else I've met. She got to know them well by finding ways to win them over and find—or create—common ground.

Kathy had the unique ability to identify introverts versus extroverts, and sort out the detailer versus the generalist. She could identify client trademarks and had the unique ability to know how and where to steer the relationship. This chapter will identify some of these customer personalities and discuss ways to deal with them.

Clients form and exhibit traits from multiple types of patterns. One of the most popular programs I have delivered over the years is a presentation titled "X-Raying the Prospects." In this seminar, we examine the characteristics of some 28 different personality patterns and provide various methods on how to deal with them.

NAPOLEON THE STRUTTER: THE BANTAM ROOSTER

Napoleon the Strutter is our first personality. We affectionately refer to this customer as the "Bantam Rooster," because they generally rub you raw. They get a kick out of ruffling your feathers.

The great temptation is to put Napoleons in their place, because they may be wrong more than they are right. Because the "strutter" is self-centered, they will tend to brag a lot. So play to their personality. Compliment Napoleon often. Stroke his ego. Prop him up. It'll be much easier solving their problem if they see you as an ally.

NO-NO NED: THE NEVER-NEVER CLIENT

"No-No Ned" can be a problem customer. The "Neds" of the world never agree to anything. They suffer from "oppositional reflex," that is, they take the opposite position on every issue. You say yes; they say no. You say black; they say white. You say day; they say night.

This customer flirts with solutions, but never seems to get there without a battle. So remain kind but forceful with them. It's okay to close hard on solutions because they get a kick out of taking the opposite position on everything you propose. You may have to spend lots of time dealing with "No-No Ned" if you expect to satisfy them. In some cases, you are better off "firing the client" if they insist on demanding that you deliver the impossible.

HARD-NOSED HARRY: THE TOUGH GUY

"Hard-Nosed Harry" is one difficult guy. This customer is genuinely baffling because of an unyielding personality. The best piece of advice I can offer is to ignore his act, because that's all it is: an act. He uses it because it works so well on people.

Harry uses his tough-guy image to scare people off, so try killing this customer with kindness. Adopt the philosophy: "Be wrong so that Harry may be right." Earn their trust, and the Harrys of the world will buy much from you.

MANNY-THE-MILQUETOAST: TIMID TOMMY

"Manny-the-Milquetoast" is like a little Timid Tommy—afraid of everyone and everything. The great temptation is to bully Tommy into doing anything you want. Because of their timidity, it's easy to try to push them around—but don't do it. Instead, keep your promises to this apprehensive prospect. They might be "Milquetoast," but they have feelings and deserve to be treated fairly and decently. Compliment the shy prospect, but be sincere with them. They wear their feelings right on their sleeve. Work closely with them for solutions that are fair and equitable and they will refer others to you because you were so patient.

JERRY THE JESTER: THE WISECRACK ARTIST

The Jester is a joker who is full of themselves. They have an abundance of wit and wisdom that they will freely share with you whether you want to hear it or not. They love to joke around, many times at your expense. The tricks and pranks they will play with you are all about subterfuge.

The Jester likes to cheat and plot. They are not terribly honest, though they appear very candid. Do not contradict them; that means that you are playing their game. You can flatter the Jester into almost any decision to buy into any proposal you suggest.

One effective method is to use closed-ended questions that start with the words "did, would, could, should, may, and can." Typically, since these questions lead to yes-no responses, they'll allow you to channel and direct them toward a decision.

NORRIS THE NAÏVE: THE UNTRIED, INEXPERIENCED CLIENT

The "naïve" client is typically young and inexperienced and doesn't have a lot of skill in dealing with important decisions. Counsel with them; let them benefit from your know-how and your ability to solve their problems.

Never take advantage of the untried client. Their immaturity is not a trait for you to exploit, but rather to understand. They respect your opinion and will do a lot of business with you if you'll simply treat them fairly and honestly. Like all babes in the woods, they occasionally need a pacifier. Pacify them and they will not only do business with you, but they'll refer their friends. Violate their trust, and you will lose them forever!

MIDDLE-AGED MAX: THE LARGEST CUSTOMER BASE

Middle-Aged Maxes are the largest of the customer base today and the most active of all the age-groups. Their age range is typically 30 to 55 and they are the target of most of the advertising done today because they buy the bulk of new homes, cars, and other major purchases. Statistically, they constitute close to half the buying public. They change jobs more often than other groups. They are much more transitional in that they have kids and their circumstances are in a constant state of flux.

Max is not necessarily the most accomplished or affluent of all clients, but he *is* the largest segment of the buying public. Despite the fact that they are still blossoming as customers, they have, nevertheless, accomplished much in their adult life. This group is very conscious of peer pressure, so compliment them often on these issues and you will be engaging a customer for life.

ALBERT THE AGED: THE OLDER PROSPECT

Though my grandfather died at the age of 60, I recall thinking that he was an old man. The fact was, even in that era, 60 was not considered "old." The good news is we're living longer. The bad news . . . we're living longer. Many retirees today will spend as much time in their retirement years as they did in their working years. In some countries, it's even

common for people to enter their retirement in their early 50s.

The older generation—or "baby boom-
ers," as they have been labeled—happens
to be the best heeled of all the demograph-
ics. Many spent the first 18 years of their
married life raising children and now find
themselves spending the same amount of
time taking care of elderly parents.

This generation likes to see the paperwork. My Uncle George Renard was a World
War II veteran who told the greatest war sto-
ries I ever heard—and had the paperwork to back them up. He actually
could back the stories up with documents and facts. "You can't tell the
story unless you have the paperwork to support it," explained my uncle.

So ask Albert's advice; get his opinion; and respect his views. This generation has become increasingly "wary" due to reversals in their invest-
ments over the years and children becoming ever more dependent upon
them. Give them the respect they have earned with their time invested
on this planet. They will appreciate your courtesy toward them.

THE DEAN OF MEAN: THE FORCEFUL BUYER

The Dean of Mean is usually a large,
forceful client who really gets a kick out of
throwing their weight around. Since they
are large and direct people, they are accus-
tomed to getting their way.

The forceful buyer is not too deep of
a thinker. You will be tempted to fight
back. Don't do it. That's exactly what they
are seeking—because they're looking forward to beating you up.

Instead, let them win on inconsequen-
tial points that do not matter. Use the

"take away close." The reason this closing technique works so well is simple: "They want what they cannot have."

Practice this on your fellow salespeople or on your kids. Give them three options, two of which you know they want and one that is only so/so—then take that one away. Guess which one they will cry over? Taking it away will cause them to be even more interested in that which they cannot have.

Finally and most important, do not back down from the forceful buyer. The moment you do, you have lost any credibility and any respect they may have had for you.

MOUTHY MALCOLM: THE TALKATIVE CUSTOMER

Perhaps the most frustrating clients we deal with are those who simply won't shut up: the talkative customers. Not that you have much choice, but try to develop good listening habits with these clients. You can't out-talk them so don't try. Appeal to this characteristic that they have in their personality. Give them feedback. "If I understand you correctly, Mr. Client, you're saying. . . ." Then paraphrase their comments and write them down to make sure you have quoted them accurately.

Play to their strengths. Use open-ended questions that are designed to elicit a rhetorical, open-ended response. Let them talk, but find a place to cap and channel the conversation. Otherwise, they'll simply talk you out of the proposal before you've had a chance to conclude it.

When they take that big breath to gain new strength to continue their verbal barrage, hop in and say something creative like, "You said something just then . . ." They'll freeze in their tracks. They can't wait to hear what you think they said that is so important—mostly because they know they haven't said anything of significance in years. They'll pause to hear what you have to say.

DOBIE THE DOUBTER: THE SKEPTICAL CLIENT

Dobie the Doubters are skeptical people who don't trust you. By nature, they are rational folks who are generally nonbelievers. Perhaps they have been burned before and they want to avoid a replay.

Help comfort them by isolating their objections. Try to zero in on the real issues and avoid emotion. Do not let them introduce evidence of another occasion that has nothing to do with the issues at hand.

Try using the Ben Franklin close. It's a simple process that has been around for hundreds of years. Draw a line down the middle of a piece of paper. Write the word *good* on one side and *bad* on the other.

GOOD	BAD

Volunteer the negatives; narrow the objections; and isolate the issues. By now, the client has already expressed their thoughts, so put them on the table first. "If I understood you correctly, Mr. and Ms. Client, you said, ..." Write them down on the negative side.

On the positive side, make a list of all the attributes your proposal espouses. If the Doubters are as rational as you perceive, they will see your longer list as ample reason to accept your proposal. Logic and rationality should win out.

Finally, be aware of the authority that exists in silence. Know when to shut up. There is power in what Paul Harvey used to call the "pregnant pause." Stop talking and simply look them in the eye.

FLAWLESS FRANCIS: THE PRECISION PROSPECT

Flawless Francis is the precision buyer, the perfectionist, the client for whom everything must be perfect or they refuse to proceed. They are analytical in their approach to everything. "Flawless" likes details and will often make decisions based on those meticulous facts that have little to do with the overall decision. They are sticklers for particulars and they love "third-party proof" that verifies their position.

Letters of recommendation from similar prospects are particularly helpful with "Flawless Francis." Do not rush Francis; if this client feels pushed, she'll likely turn and run. Take the time to educate and motivate them with the facts.

APATHETIC ALEX: THE INDIFFERENT PROSPECT

Apathetic Alex is just plain bored. Their apathy speaks to their tremendous indifference toward everything you are proposing. At best, these clients are "lukewarm" about every suggestion you make. They will often yawn or look away as if you're killing them with boredom. It's as if they don't want to be there.

Though they tend to look permanently unconcerned, nonchalant, and even unbiased, don't buy it. It's part of their act. Instead, draw them out with open-ended questions that will encourage them to provide you with key information that can assist you in solving their problem.

Close them early and often. Don't be afraid to use visual aids and third-party testimonials to make key points—and be sure to cover those "hot button" questions.

HEADSTRONG HENRY: THE STUBBORN PROSPECT

Hanks are just plain stubborn! They are dogmatic, contentious, narrow-minded, and unshakable in their beliefs. Compliment them with firm resolve. Be careful not to confuse them with the facts. These folks buy based on emotion, not logic.

The business goes on the books on the shoulders of an emotional decision. However, make no mistake; it stays on the books with logic. Don't get into a verbal volleyball game with Henry. He's headstrong and proud of it.

Be careful with Henry. Don't start believing your own press releases about how great you and your company are. He's not buying it, and frankly, neither should you. It's okay to be confident in what you offer, but don't make the mistake of believing your own marketing propaganda. Keep it real with Harry—he just wants the facts.

OSCAR THE ORATOR: THE OPINIONATED CLIENT

Oscar the Orator has an opinion about everything. This prospect wants to be heard on any and all issues. They ramble a lot and rarely have a point to their conversation— so you must learn to guide their discourse and bring them back to the subject at hand. Ask lots of questions, but always direct the conversation.

Oscar is going to need to have the last word. Let it go. Close hard and often on minor points. Keep Oscar on track. Understand that, like most people, Oscar does and says things for his reasons, not for yours. Find out what motivates Oscar and appeal to that.

SASSY STANLEY: THE SARDONIC SLOB

Stanley knows it all and he enjoys being sassy about it all. As the old saying goes, any defendant who represents himself has a fool for a client. Still, you must appeal to Stanley's ego—so flatter his toughness. Use the power of silence. Speak in quiet, restrained tones. Escort them delicately through the entire process by educating them and quietly nudging them into the right decision.

LOUIE THE LIAR: PINOCCHIO

Louie can be a particularly vicious prospect. His dishonesty, conniving, corruptness, and shifty approach to everything makes this client particularly deceitful and deceptive. You run the risk of investing a lot of time in Pinocchio and having literally nothing to show for it. Discount Louie's statements. Review the facts and constantly reiterate them to Pinocchio. "You said, did you not . . ." or "I understood you to say. . . ." Put them on the spot—or be prepared to burn a lot of time with little return on your investment.

THE VERBAL SIGNS OF A LIAR:

1. They use a lot of qualifying statements and modifiers like "You follow?" or "Are you with me?" to justify their positions.
2. They make comments like "To be 100 percent honest with you, as far as I know," which suggests that they haven't been totally honest up until this point.
3. They make Freudian slips in speech patterns.
4. They change thoughts in the middle of a statement.
5. They tend to use speech patterns laced with ahh's and uhm's and you-knows. This is not simply a crying need for a Toastmasters Club; it's also an identifier of deceit.
6. They tend to stammer and stutter often.

GABBY THE GOSSIP: THE TALKER

Gabby loves to yak on the phone. This client has great verbal skills and is very articulate. They enjoy creating enthusiasm but can waste an inordinate amount of your time. Restrict and steer Gabby's conversation, or plan to spend a lot of time with her. Stick with closed-end questions. Paraphrasing might encourage Gabby to take off into different directions, so be careful to stay focused. Try to summarize and don't be afraid to use reflective silence.

PAINLESS PETER: THE EASY BUYER

Painless Peter is the easy buyer; in fact, he just may be the easiest buyer you'll ever deal with. Peter makes quick decisions, quite often without all the facts. While he is open-minded, his decisions are largely based on emotion instead of logic. These purchasers are risk-takers to some degree, which suggests that they are bored with things and don't mind making quick, miscalculated decisions based on impulsive characteristics. They often throw caution to the wind.

Peter's greatest attribute is his trusting personality, so make sure you don't abuse your relationship Painless Peter. Be totally honest and aboveboard on all issues. Treat Peter like your own parents.

RIGHT-WING RALPH: THE CONSERVATIVE PROSPECT

Ralph is a little to the right of Genghis Khan. He's a classic conservative, so do not try to change him. After all, conservatives believe they have something to conserve. Use third-party proof stories with Ralph to gain his respect of the conservative. Prove your worth to the conservative client by being true to your values and your word.

ANALYTICAL ANDY: THE LOGICAL CLIENT

Analytical Andy is a classic logical prospect who wants all the T's crossed and the I's dotted—so make sure you do it for him. Andy never buys based on emotion—only on logic. He is nearly completely concerned with profit, terms, conditions.

Avoid confusing, illogical behavior. Andy is looking for answers based on "just the facts." Avoid surprises and establish everything on terms and conditions that you can prove. Unfortunately, Andy also suffers from paralysis by analysis.

BUFORD THE BEWILDERED: THE CONFUSED CUSTOMER

Buford the Bewildered is, quite simply, confused. He doesn't know what he doesn't know and doesn't even know the right questions to ask to get the answers he needs. The best defense for this kind of perplexed prospect is his constant puzzlement; so help Buford sort things out. Ask lots of open-ended questions and let him provide the conversation's direction. Understand that Buford doesn't know his script, so lend a hand by asking the right questions and channeling his responses.

TOBY THE TEARJERKER: THE PASSIONATE CLIENT

Toby is the passionate, emotional prospect. All of his decisions are based on emotion, and he is completely indifferent to logic. Toby responds best to greed, pride, fear, and ego. Emotional clients are often spur-of-the-moment purchasers who love deals. An important characteristic is that they enjoy doing business with people they like. Warm up to Toby, and build a deep relationship with him. Appeal to his emotional side by expressing exactly what it is about your product that will make him happier/more relaxed/ more effective.

LET'S-MAKE-HIM-AN-OFFER LANCE: THE BARGAIN BUYER

The bargain buyer is always looking for a deal and will generally walk if they don't get it. Lance wants the lowest price, the best terms, the most favorable conditions—and he wants it "yesterday."

Since Lance cares only about getting the cheapest price, make room to give and take with him. Let the bargain buyer feel they are getting the best deal possible. Position yourself accordingly with Lance, and you'll save time and resources.

MICROSCOPIC MELVIN: THE RATIONAL BUYER

This may be the most rational person with whom you will ever come in contact. Paying meticulous attention to every detail, Melvin doesn't miss anything. These buyers gravitate to certain professions, such as accounting, planning, and engineering. The nature of their work suggests that they are drawn to analytical work. Save tons of time by providing Melvin with all the facts. The rational buyer will not proceed without them.

WISHY-WASHY WOODY: THE INDECISIVE CLIENT

Woody will make you crazy if you let him, because this client is incredibly indecisive. They are often uninformed and will vacillate between decisions. When dealing with this type of customer, close on every key point and close often. Isolate his objections.

A very effective approach to working with the indecisive client is to use the "set aside" close. Identify the major problems, and set them aside. Once you've cleared up all the other issues, come back to what you've "set aside" and deal with it.

ORNERY OLIN: THE OBSTINATE BUYER

Ornery Olin is an obstinate client who has many of the same characteristics of several of the others on our list. He is indecisive and many times uninformed. It's completely fair to have an agreement with the Olin on the front end to set the terms and conditions of your relationship. Bring the agreement up as often as necessary.

The Olins of the world fluctuate often; they simply will not make decisions. Close them on every key point and remind them of their agreement. Isolate the objections. Set them aside and come back and close on the isolated areas.

TAKEAWAY SERVICING AND SELLING TACTICS
LISTEN
1. Keep an open mind.
2. Consider how all customer service tools may be used by you to improve your business.
3. Profile your customer to know their characteristics.

LEARN
1. Increase your library of resources.
2. Plan your strategy.
3. Know the characteristics of your client.

LEAD THE CUSTOMER TO SOLUTIONS
1. Create the environment.
2. Introduce the vision.
3. Communicate the expectations.
4. Help your client find answers to their questions.

CHAPTER 17

FIND OUT WHAT THE CUSTOMERS NEED AND GIVE IT TO THEM

Customers dictate winners and losers.

There is wide variety of reasons that customers crown you king or queen of their domain. From the vendor's standpoint, you need to quickly identify those reasons and go "Minnesota Fats" as quickly as possible. Minnesota Fats was a famous pool shark who never broke the rack without knowing where all of his next shots would be. "Fats" could see what did not exist just yet: his last shot for the game win.

While most of us in the business world don't have to possess that kind of acumen, there is one simple thing we can do: Find out what the customers want, and give it to them. Unfortunately, most companies simply want to dump what they have on their shelves rather than asking customers about their needs before even building the widget.

I spoke to a group of colleges and universities that are part of a consortium that develops and shares software to help them navigate through the maze of new problems they now face. These issues range from HIPAA regulations, to processing credit and debit cards, to taking on the role of student loan administrators. New requirements fall to them daily, and new headaches accompany those obligations.

The biggest challenges that all universities face are the bulging enrollments that are impregnated by record unemployment and layoffs in the corporate world. People are using this downtime to reload their guns and acquire skills that will make them more marketable in the ever-changing workplace.

That's the good news for all these schools, particularly community-based commuter colleges. The huge influx of people is those folks living at home and driving down to the local campus to pick up valuable courses.

The bad news is that these schools had a need for virtual classrooms yesterday. They simply don't have the brick and mortar to accommodate enrollments that have skyrocketed to 125 percent of capacity in some cases. Moreover, they don't have the funding and staffing to deal with the overwhelming enrollments.

For instance, demand for the sciences is higher than ever, and while virtual classrooms are part of the solution, they simply need more lab space for people to pursue these disciplines. That takes time and money. Had these institutions anticipated this demand, they might be better equipped to make this transition. The problem is they were so busy filling the space they had that they failed to go "Minnesota Fats" and anticipate where they needed to be.

FIND OUT WHAT THE CUSTOMER NEEDS AND THEN GIVE IT TO THEM

Who is the real customer in this university scenario? If you're thinking it's the student, you're wrong. It's the end employer who is going to hire these wayward students. This is the customer who will crown the king.

Forward-thinking businesses anticipate the needs well in advance of the problem and position themselves to solve it. That requires these vendors to reduce the complexity of the process and integrate services with ease and minimal delay. The problem that most corporations, associations, churches, and other institutions have is moving from the "insight" stage to the "integration" stage. They have terrific ideas but cannot implement them.

One of the challenges that the consortium of universities faces is that many of their members already have the answers but are buried deep within their own "silos." If university "A" could share how it solved its HIPAA and credit card/debit card compliance issue with university "B," it could save them a tremendous amount of time, talent, and treasure. However, the forum to do so is simply not in place, and meeting every few years to network the ideas isn't going to get the job done. These folks are so busy doing their jobs that they haven't taken the time to find out how others are doing the same things better, quicker, and more cheaply.

If the people buried in these silos would simply conduct a one hour WEB-EX or Go To Meeting session per week, they could increase their learning curve significantly with the investment of a mere hour. There are countless other social media methods available to dispense this kind of information. You simply have to decide which one works best for you and your purposes, and master its use accordingly.

Working with an existing network of people with the same problems is what associations and consortiums of this nature are all about. Optimizing it into the marketplace is somewhat tougher to do. These third party solutions and applications can trim the learning curve significantly and save money. They operate in a mutual environment with mutual problems. There may be deployment issues that range from institution "A" to institution "B," but that stuff is about the process and can easily be addressed.

If the endgame here is to get these new college entrants trained to get back into the workplace and better equipped intellectually, then every step of that process—from getting them into the right curriculum to paying for it—should be addressed. This is how you protect your existing investment and innovate for the future, and always be thinking like "Minnesota Fats."

TAKEAWAY SERVICING AND SELLING TACTICS

1. Discover who the real customer is.
2. Investigate what their real needs are, and then find out how to fill them.
3. Try to anticipate future issues and problems, and "solve" them before they arise.

CHAPTER 18

FIND OUT WHAT OTHERS ARE DOING AND DO SOMETHING DIFFERENT!

My twin sons were born on July 28, 1978, and I was facing a critical decision. I had just won the regional championship level of the World Championship of Public Speaking for Toastmasters International in Norfolk, Virginia, several weeks before, and I had a decision to make. If my sons were not born before I was to leave, I would have to forfeit my position and have a surrogate replace me in Vancouver, British Columbia, Canada.

The decision was made somewhat easier when Christine delivered a bit early. Now I had another decision to make: Do I abandon her with newborn twins to chase this dream of winning a World Championship of Public Speaking?

That decision was simplified with the arrival of a pair of grandmothers and another half dozen aunts, all of whom wanted a piece of the action. I had trouble getting seat time with my own twin sons.

Realizing this, Christine banished and shipped me off to Vancouver with a simple dictate: Win or don't come home! No pressure there.

I had already blown this same championship the year before in Toronto, Ontario, by going eight seconds over my allotted time limit, thereby getting disqualified. I learned this after I was told that I had

119

won. "Oops, we need that trophy back, big boy. You went a tad long, eh?" I didn't appreciate the Canadian "eh" postscript.

So I landed in British Columbia with this new dictate from my bride . . . to win or don't come home. My first inclination was to find a specialty shop and have a trophy made up that said 1978 World Champion Speaker, but my hypocrisy only goes so far.

The Toastmasters International Convention is a weeklong gala that culminates with the World Championship on Saturday morning.

The entire convention is composed of two elements of people. The first are those political animals that venture through the process of running for international director. These folks remind me a lot of Trekkies, who have never missed a Star Trek convention. They are single-minded in their purpose. Some haven't missed a Toastmasters Convention in 40 years.

And then there's the other element like yours truly, who has no interest in letters after their name or holding office or becoming anything other than a better speaker. We are a minority at these conventions, but a respected minority nevertheless.

Since I had blown it the previous year by going a lousy eight seconds over my time limit, the word was out that "Stupid was back for another go at it."

Interestingly, I got a standing ovation during that speech in Toronto, Ontario, in 1977. It lasted eight seconds. Duh! Determined not to make that same mistake twice, I decided that I needed to focus on two things: (1) Finish on time, and (2) find a way to be different.

The World Championship of Public Speaking features all nine regional finalists from throughout the Toastmasters International speaking world, representing about a quarter million members from over 100 countries worldwide.

The judges meet with you prior to the contest to review the rules and to remind dummies like yours truly not to go over the time limit. By the time you reach the finals, you have already mailed in all the copies of your previous speeches, none of which can be similar in any way. After the district level of competition, you are required to write and submit a new and different presentation at each new level.

So I had the time thing down pat this go around after screwing up royally the previous year. Next, I had to find a way to be different. When we drew straws, I learned I would speak last. I immediately called Christine to tell her I was about to win. "How do you know that?" she queried. All I had to do was watch the first eight and find a way to be different. I did just that.

I'm told by Terry McCann, the late executive director of Toastmasters International, that I was the first speaker in the history of the competition to venture out from behind the podium.

It startled some and amazed others, and I suspect it clearly gave me the winning edge. So my advice to people today is simple: Find out what everybody else is doing . . . then do something different. That's pretty good advice in life if you think about it.

Toastmasters International has made me a lot of money over my four decades in business. Granted, it improved my speaking skills and introduced me to a speaking career. However, that was not my initial goal. I actually wanted to be a better salesperson and I realized that in order to do that I would have to improve my communication skills.

The Knights of Columbus Insurance promoted me to General Agent in Central Florida in 1989. Every single agent I've hired since the day I took over has been given the same advice: Join Toastmasters. It is the single quickest way I know of to improve your communication skills.

When my client Patrick Callahan told me in 1974 that he could "shop" his insurance, I was so desperate to hang onto a new client that I asked the question: "When do we meet?"

TAKEAWAY SERVICING AND SELLING TACTICS

1. In order to be a more effective communicator, you should join Toastmasters. Not only will it improve your communication skills, but you'll learn valuable lessons about leadership and listening.
2. Leaders all over the world have professed their appreciation for Toastmasters and sing the organization's praises.
3. Not only will you learn how to more effectively communicate, Toastmasters will also teach you how to be a better listener.
4. You will improve your presentation skills while gaining valuable confidence; that will make you better at everything you do.

CHAPTER 19

BECOME A MENTOR TO YOUR CLIENT; COACH AND COUNSEL!

Are you a helicopter, a drill sergeant, or a coach?

One of my favorite presentations that I deliver dozens of times each year is a program I've titled "Helicopters, Drill Sergeants, or Coaches . . . Which Are You?" In short, there are three kinds of salespeople, customer service representatives, parents, and leaders. Despite the title you have, the way in which you interact with others can usually be distilled down to one of these three categories. This chapter will examine how each one works with the people with whom you interact.

Let it be said at the outset that we all possess the qualities of all three of these styles described in this chapter. The following quiz will help you assess which style is most like your own. Assess yourself to see where you stand.

1. Almost all people could improve their job performance quite a bit if they really wanted to.

Strongly Disagree	Disagree	Agree	Strongly Agree

2. It's unrealistic to expect people to show the same enthusiasm for their work as for their leisure activities.

Strongly Disagree	Disagree	Agree	Strongly Agree

3. Even when they receive encouragement from the boss, very few people show the desire to improve themselves on the job.

Strongly Disagree	Disagree	Agree	Strongly Agree

4. If you give people enough money, they are less likely to worry about such intangibles as status or recognition.

Strongly Disagree	Disagree	Agree	Strongly Agree

5. When people talk about wanting more responsibility in their jobs, they really mean more money and an elevated status.

Strongly Disagree	Disagree	Agree	Strongly Agree

6. Because most people don't like to make decisions on their own, it's hard to get them to assume responsibility.

Strongly Disagree	Disagree	Agree	Strongly Agree

7. Being tough with people usually gets them to do what you want.

Strongly Disagree	Disagree	Agree	Strongly Agree

8. A good way to get people to do more work is to crack down on them once in a while.

Strongly Disagree	Disagree	Agree	Strongly Agree

9. It weakens a person's prestige when they have to admit that a subordinate was right and they were wrong.

Strongly Disagree	Disagree	Agree	Strongly Agree

10. The most effective supervisors, leaders, customer service representatives, or parents are the ones who get expected results, regardless of the methods they use in handling people.

Strongly Disagree	Disagree	Agree	Strongly Agree

11. It's too much to expect that people will try doing a good job without being prodded by their superior.

Strongly Disagree	Disagree	Agree	Strongly Agree

12. The superior who expects people to set their own standards for superior performance will probably find they don't set them very high.

Strongly Disagree	Disagree	Agree	Strongly Agree

13. If people do not use much imagination and ingenuity on the job, it is probably because relatively few people have much of either.

Strongly Disagree	Disagree	Agree	Strongly Agree

14. One problem with asking for ideas from subordinates is that their perspective is too limited for their suggestions to be of much practical value.

Strongly Disagree	Disagree	Agree	Strongly Agree

15. It's human nature for people to try to do as little work as they can get away with.

Strongly Disagree	Disagree	Agree	Strongly Agree

1. TOTAL FOR COLUMNS

Strongly Disagree	Disagree	Agree	Strongly Agree

2. ABOVE TOTALS

Strongly Disagree	Disagree	Agree	Strongly Agree
× 1	× 2	× 3	× 4

3. GRAND TOTAL

Strongly Disagree	Disagree	Agree	Strongly Agree

1. Total each column.
2. Multiply each column by the specified multiplier.
3. Add all column totals.
4. Your answer should be somewhere between 15 and 60.
5. Carry these figures down and add them across.

If your scores fall between 45 and 60, you are more of a Drill Sergeant. If your scores fall in the middle, you are more of a Helicopter. If you score in the final third, you are a Coach or a Counselor in your style.

DRILL SERGEANTS

Drill Sergeants are process-oriented people and autocratic leaders. Often, they have closed communication and are almost secretive in nature. The autocrat believes that people are motivated by fear of punishment. They place emphasis on control procedures and techniques for counseling with people on what to do and how to do it.

These individuals work best with people who are dependent on them with little expression or interaction with others. These individuals love to issue orders and expect others to jump when they say jump.

The autocrat is always "in charge" and a bit of a control freak. They often micromanage situations and people and are seen as a "bully" by others. Like their military counterparts, Drill Sergeants love to make demands and dictates such as "It's my way or the highway." These folks are stubborn and often wrong.

The nature of the Drill Sergeant is that of an obsessive-compulsive person who offers no choice. "You'll do it my way or else!" Drill Sergeants reach decisions without consulting others—and often create levels of discontent in the process.

HELICOPTERS

If your score falls between 15 and 30, you are a Helicopter or have a humanistic style. These folks are extremely "people oriented." They love open communication and direct response from others. The Helicopter is more of a democratic style whose nature invites others' opinions and often seeks a seemingly impossible consensus. It is particularly problematic when there is a wide range of options and no clear way of reaching an equitable and final decision; then, chaos often reigns.

It is Helicopters' sincere belief that people find their work satisfying and that they voluntarily seek responsibility. The humanistic interaction technique emphasizes the nature of relationships and the creation of an environment that encourages support for the company's goals.

The Helicopter promotes group decision making whenever possible. They work best with self-reliant, experienced workers who are "can-do" people who can make decisions. However, Helicopters tend to hover and protect those with whom they work. One of their problems is they are much like the big oak tree in that nothing grows under it. Its protective strength becomes its inherent weakness.

I often refer to the Helicopter style as "the rescuer." They are always bailing others out and never holding them accountable for anything.

COACHES

If your score falls between 30 and 45, you are a Coach or a Counselor. Coaches possess a mixture of the characteristics of both the Helicopter and the Drill Sergeant. They are fond of giving people choices and like to hold people accountable, but they take the time to educate people on the choices they make.

The Coach uses a teamwork approach to everything and believes that teams work best when they have common commitments to actions involved in relevant decision making. Instead of being competitive, team members are collaborative when working toward joint goals. In the end, several people working together can make better decisions than one person alone.

Participative styles avoid the autocratic kinds of decisions the Drill Sergeant likes to make. Instead, they seek the opinions of subordinates, peers, superiors, and other stakeholders, such as the customer. However, if not checked and managed correctly, the influence peddler might take control over the whole spectrum.

Coaches are concerned (as well they should be) with high standards. The breakdown comes in communicating the standards to the parties. In a perfect world, everyone would know their own script and would follow it accordingly, working toward the common goal of what is best for the majority. Here's where a touch of authoritarianism is needed to channel the results into a positive win–win solution.

The key to good coaching: Give people choices.

TAKEAWAY SERVICING AND SELLING TACTICS

1. Avoid being a Drill Sergeant who demands that you do it your way or no way.
2. Avoid being the Helicopter who always hovers and protects, never letting anyone take responsibility for their own actions.
3. Seek to be a coach. Like counselors and mentors, they educate people and encourage them to make their own decisions.

CHAPTER 20

WINNING IS NEVER FINAL AND LOSING IS NEVER FATAL

Stuff is going to go wrong, so get over it. Fix it and move on, and above all, be thankful. This is a gift that keeps on giving. The key is to get people to fail faster.

Some customers are like porcupines: You just can't pet them. You can't please them. You can't console them. But they are a gift that keeps on giving because they offer us challenges that other, more agreeable customers don't.

If it's understood that in order to have more success in life we need more failure, we therefore should teach people to "fail faster." You don't necessarily have to get "good" at it—but don't be afraid to get past the problem. While loyalty is a gift that keeps on giving, frustrating customers are also a gift that can pay you big dividends. Customer loyalty can be defined in many ways. One of the best: The one who fixes the problem gets the biz!

I have been an agent with the Knights of Columbus Insurance for nearly four decades. We actually have clients who own 40 to 50 contracts on themselves and members of their family. We know that happy members are 12 percent more likely to add more business simply because they are so pleased with our ratings and service. We know also that we close 26 percent of all new prospects on whom we call. We're aware of these statistics because I've been keeping score on them for the past 20-plus years. For instance, we know that 41 percent of the people we talk to on the phone will say, "Sure, come on out." And 25 percent of the folks we interview will buy something from us. These are our averages, for better or worse.

If we fall below those ratios, I have reason to be concerned.

IT'S THE SERVICE, STUPID!

You have to work hard to maintain and build on customer loyalty. When Knights of Columbus members abandon their business with the Order, more often than not, it wasn't the price that was wrong; it was something that we did or failed to do for the member. We control our own destiny. And when we occasionally fail, it is because of a policy decision or our inability to perform in the eyes of our members. We have to be accountable.

VALUES DRIVE DECISIONS

Many years ago, the Knights of Columbus made a conscious decision to avoid selling certain products that had a higher than normal element of risk associated with them. It didn't make these products bad products, but since our members don't desire these kinds of risk, we simply didn't offer them. If a client doesn't fully understand a product, then the responsibility for explaining this falls to the company. In simple terms, we determined that our clients don't want to have to figure that stuff out. They want guarantees—so that's exactly what we offer them. Our values are clear, so that decision came easily. And that's why there are less than a handful of companies in the world who have our safety ratings.

TAKEAWAY SERVICING AND SELLING TACTICS
1. Customer loyalty is earned and maintained through integrity.
2. When we do fail, we need to hold ourselves accountable.
3. Your company needs to maintain its values in order to keep its customers.

CHAPTER 21

MASTER YOUR TIME OR IT WILL ENSLAVE YOU

Time, both yours and theirs: Master it or it will master you.

If you were given $86,400 every day and told to invest it wisely or lose it, you would treat the process very seriously, would you not? If you were rewarded $31,536,000 tax-free this year and told, "Use it or lose it," hopefully, you would become a good steward of those funds in the truest sense of the word.

Each of us begins our day with an identical number of minutes: 1,440. We are each awarded 86,400 seconds when the clock hits 12:00 AM Why is it that some of us spend that judiciously and others waste it? I suspect there are hundreds of reasons.

Both you and your client have more valuable things to do with your time than to waste it on unproductive matters and conversations. One of the biggest complaints that customers lodge is the *time* they have to waste to get a problem rectified.

You may be fabulous at the client service you render, but if you're a lousy manager of your most valuable resource — time — then all could be lost for naught. It starts with better organization and clear-cut priorities. Eliminate the time robbers that rip away at your schedule like hungry piranha.

In my nearly four decades in the insurance industry, I have concluded that there are scores of "time thieves" that attack us and our clients on a daily basis. They range from uninvited drop-ins to unwelcome e-mails, from junk mail to the piles of regulatory rubbish that has inundated our industry.

All of this flak is what we have to navigate through to win the time wars every day. It's not easy, but the purpose of this chapter is to help you address some of the most common ones.

SNAIL MAIL

Both you and your clients get your share of junk snail mail every day, despite the fact that the post office has changed their rates so often that they have introduced the "*forever*" stamp. What do you do with all the stuff that comes across your desk every day? Sometimes I think our home office is killing at least one forest per week, and our company isn't an exception. Your clients may be opening your mail, but they too have been so inundated that they pitch it before you can even earn a glance-over.

When I first got into the business, our insurance application was a mere two pages. Now, we actually have a booklet that is literally 26 pages long—which doesn't even include HIPAA or special beneficiary designation forms. Somebody invented a cruel joke when they coined the term *paperless office*. When our clients see me whip out the booklet, they look at me with this forlorn expression: "Wonder how long this is going to take?"

We can't do much about those things that are thrust on us by the powers that be like the IRS and city hall. We *can* do something about how we handle this forest that hits our desk. Here are the four Aun Rules to live by:

Aun Rule Number 1: Handle the paper *only once*.

Aun Rule Number 2: If you pick it up, review it, and don't make a decision on what to do with it, fold a corner. If you pick it up again, fold another corner. If you pick it up again, fold another corner. Four corners ought to give you a clue about what to do with the document.

Aun Rule Number 3: Make a decision. Carnegie said, "If you're right 51 percent of the time, you'll be a winner." The number one problem facing middle management today is to get people to make decisions.

Aun Rule Number 4: "Ready, Fire, Aim." So what if you screw up— just MAKE A DECISION! Ben Franklin did something in his day that I find interesting, even by today's standards. He would not open his mail for weeks at a time. By the time he got around to opening it, most of the problems had solved themselves.

E-MAIL

Get a good spam-blocker on your computer to keep unsolicited or unwanted e-mail from taking over your life. Because I have a number of web sites, I get about a thousand-plus such e-mails daily, but my spam-blocker system catches most of them.

Don't waste your time trying to set up blocking mechanisms. For each one you establish, there are dozens of ways around them. If someone wants to communicate badly enough with you, they can request admittance into your phone book. You at least get to review their e-mail in your suspect spam folder before having to admit them.

PEOPLE DROPPING IN ON YOU, VIRTUALLY OR IN PERSON

Everybody needs rules; without them, it would be incredibly hard to stay in business. One of my rules is that I will only see salespeople in my office from 5:00 AM–7:00 AM on Fridays.

If you want to sell me something, that's when I buy. My office, my rules. I'm very attentive and most times I'll buy from someone who is selling something I want. However, the pitch is over at 7:00 AM sharp—no exceptions. If the person with whom I'm meeting isn't done, they have to come back next Friday. These parameters help move the meeting along and encourage people to address issues in a concise manner. Additionally, I know that only the people who genuinely want my attention will show up (after all, getting up at 5 AM is no easy task for some of us!).

HAVE YOU GOT A MINUTE?

I'd like to have a quarter for every time someone said, "Have you got a minute?" I'd be a wealthy man. These are the four steps I use to respond to that query:

1. "If it really will only take a minute."
2. Always stand; never sit. It's too uncomfortable for people to rob you from a standing position.
3. I take off my watch and look at it with one eye and them with the other.
4. When the minute is up, I move on. No exceptions.

MYTHS ABOUT NEEDING OR WANTING MORE TIME

In a survey for an audio training system that I produced titled "Winning the Time Wars," I found that 40 percent of the people I surveyed say they need about 25 percent more time. Some 50 percent of the people in the survey said they actually needed 50 percent more time. There are many myths in time management, some of which include:

The myth of time shortage, that is, the contention that no one has enough time. Though people constantly make this claim, we all have the same amount. Time is not the problem; it's how we use the limited supply that is. Learn to just say no. Confusing priorities cause problems, the most typical of which is choosing to work on "second things" first.

The myth that time "flies" or "marches on." Actually, time stays constant. It is ever present, and always definitive. Time is not against us; usually, our own habits are.

The myth of activity. We confuse mere activity with actual achievement of substantial projects. While active people get more done, there are two kinds of "active" people: "proactive" and "reactive." You want to be "proactive."

The myth of the decision level. Some people think that the higher up in the organization a decision is made, the better the decision. This is not necessarily the case. We need to make better decisions quicker.

The myth of highly paid people, that is, people who are paid more must make smarter decisions. Since when does income dictate good decision-making skills?

The myth of the delayed decision. Does delay improve the quality of a decision? Not necessarily so; in fact, sometimes it can create a bigger problem than it solves. "Paralysis by analysis" is an accepted fact of life. Yes, you must get the facts, but then decide. You waste valuable time procrastinating decisions that are inevitable.

The myth of delegation. Delegating responsibilities and tasks to other saves time, worry, and responsibility—as long as these individuals have the capacity to complete the tasks in question. Additionally, it's best not to delegate activities that only you should be completing. Ask yourself: "Is this delegation or abdication?"

The myth of efficiency. The most efficient person is not necessarily the most effective. Don't try to do more cheaply that which should not be done at all. Effectiveness is doing the right things right. The danger in "multitasking" is that you run the risk of doing several things at once, and doing none of them well. Focus on the activities that need your full concentration; otherwise, you'll spend even more time correcting your mistakes.

The myth of omnipotence, that is, I have to do it because no one else can; only I can achieve these tasks faster and better. Perhaps, but don't do that which you can give to others to do (see "the myth of delegation"), or that which should not be done at all. They may well do it better than you, while you invest your time more wisely.

The myth of overworked executives. Clarence Randall once wrote, "Pity the overworked, disorganized martyrs." Many times, we hide behind our workload as the reasons for our failures. In reality, we're not really getting very much done; we're simply claiming that we are so that we have an excuse when certain things remain undone. Don't let the length of your "to-do" list intimidate you; break it down, and tackle it piece by piece.

The myth of the "open door." Some managers believe the open-door policy improves the effectiveness of his or her team, but more often than not, open door becomes open season. You go from being part of the solution to part of the problem. Effective managers are virtually unanimous in their desire for a quiet hour. I'm in my office by 5:00 AM every day because I want three hours of quiet time before the phone starts to ring. There's nothing wrong with having an open-door policy; just modify it a bit and have regular hours during which employees and colleagues can "drop" by, with other hours off-limits.

The myth of problem identification. Some people tend to spend an inordinate amount of time "figuring out" what the problem is. In reality, identifying the problem is the easiest part of solving it. Avoid becoming a symptom of the problem by prolonging this process; determine how to move forward as quickly as possible.

The myth of time saving. Though many shortcuts are time savers, a lot of them can also produce bigger problems. No one can elect not to spend time or to spend it at a different rate. We must expect the unexpected. You never want to cut important conversations short or hasten a decision without critical facts. If you don't have time to do something right the first time, when will you find the time to fix it?

WE ARE OUR OWN ENEMY

The great philosopher Pogo once remarked, "We have met the enemy and it is us!" Time is our scarcest resource; unless we learn to manage it, we likely cannot manage anything else. The question to ask is not "Where *does* your time go?" The correct question is "Where *should* your time go?"

SIX QUICK TIPS TO MAXIMIZE YOUR TIME

There is precious little we can do to put a stop to the things we can't control in our lives, but there are still a lot of things we can control—including how we spend (some of) our time. The following tips will make a difference in how you spend this precious commodity.

1. Turn your driving time into learning time. Turn the radio or iPod off for a while, and listen to some motivational speakers or book recordings.

2. Turn your "on hold" time into learning time. Set up a three-ring binder on your desk with all those handouts that you collect at the conferences you attend. Thumb through them as you are on hold waiting for the person on the other end to pick up. I have found I can review all my Continuing Education (CE) materials and other notes about four times a year simply while I'm on hold.

3. In the insurance industry, everybody gets "porched" from time to time; so turn this "porch time" into effective time. When it happens and you're too far from your office to return before the next appointment, pull out your database and search your client list by Zip code; then, do some "drop-in" visits. At best, it may generate more business on the spot. At worst, it should help you secure an appointment to return another time.

4. Start a daily "idea" journal, and take it everywhere you go. Take notes if you're at a standstill in traffic. Take it on your appointments. You have a daily resource bin in which to park your thoughts. A great idea can hit you at any time, so make sure you have a way to record it and use it later. I even take notes in church, which drives my priest nuts. (Every now and then he even says something worth writing down!)

5. Start folders with labels that reflect the information you wish to retain. I buy my books for this very reason. If I see something in a book or magazine I like, I tear out the pages and then file it under a category. I can then search these by topic anytime I want additional information.

6. Become a Google goony. Learn to search both ideas and graphics on search engines such as my favorite, Google. You can find terrific information under the Web topic and generic images under the Image button, such as maps, news, video, and more.

LEARN TO PRIORITIZE

We can't deflect all the "crappola" that comes our way daily, but we can make some decisions on how to process it. Social science research suggests that we can accomplish about 14 things in the course of a workday—be they appointments, phone calls, letters, or other daily business tasks.

So we have to learn to prioritize. I use a simple A-B-C-D system that works well for me. As I am building my calendar for the day to determine which 14 things I can get done, I have to make decisions on which are the most critical, and which can go undone if need be.

"A" priorities: These include appointments I've made and some important phone calls, as well as critical e-mail and snail-mail correspondence.

"B" priorities are important but not urgent; I'll do them if time permits.

"C" priorities can be done sometime this week; they are neither urgent nor important.

"D" priorities are the ones about which I'm not quite sure. We don't always know how critical they are. I use the "Four D" system. Do it, Dump it, Delay it, or Delegate it. The goal is to get it off your radar screen as soon as possible. Below is a simple matrix I use.

MICHAEL AUN PRIORITY INDEX

Level A	Urgent	Important	Must be done today
Level B	Important	Not Urgent	Could be done today if I have time
Level C	Not Urgent	Not Important	Could be done sometime this week
Level D	Not Sure	Not Sure	Do it, dump it, delay it, delegate it

ANALYZING YOUR CALENDAR

One of the best things you can do is set your major goals annually, and revisit them on a quarterly basis. This gives you a terrific opportunity to fix what needs fixing. Then, if you find that something is not working, you can quit doing it immediately.

I begin both my agency and personal yearly planning for the following year in September of each year. I use a color code system that seems to work well for me. Green days are *go* or work days. Those are the days on which I want to be in front of clients. Ideally, I want four of those days per week with a minimum of four people per day on the calendar.

Yellow days are the days I use for file preparation, paperwork, phone calling, marketing, continuing education, seminars, conventions, and any other work-related, nonselling activity.

Red days are *play* or days off. Many of these are chosen for you by custom and by choice. Typically, all the holidays are red days. Family events, birthdays, anniversaries, and vacations are also in this category for me. Some of these are up to you to decide—so choose them wisely.

Color Code	Type of Day
Green days	Work days; get in front of clients
Yellow days	File preparation, phone calling, marketing, nonselling related work activity, continuing education
Red days	Play days, days off, vacation, holidays

TAKEAWAY SERVICING AND SELLING TACTICS

1. Master your time or it will master you.
2. If it's broke, fix it. If it's not broke, break it and fix it again. There's always a better way to do it.
3. There's never a better way to do that which should not be done at all. Decide on what to do and do it. Do not delay.

CHAPTER 22

IF YOU PAY PEANUTS, YOU GET MONKEYS!

It's about the quality of those serving the customer.

I'm in the business of training people to be better at the entire customer/client service process. However, I never cease to be amazed at how much money a company will spend on marketing a product or service—and how little they invest in taking care of the client once they have made a commitment to purchase said product or service.

The billions that are lost to this flaw in the process annually are *staggering*. They are, unfortunately, also incalculable because many customers don't even bother to complain about the lousy service they got. They simply go elsewhere without saying a word.

Sadly, many companies have failed to define exactly what they want and expect from their client service reps. You certainly can't train people in a process that you haven't defined! How can you fix a problem that you refuse to acknowledge that you have?

A tremendous transformation in products has taken place over the past 40 years in the insurance industry. I have been blessed to be with the same company since I began in the field nearly 40 years ago, so my perspective is focused accordingly. Sadly, I've had a front row seat to the good, the bad, and the ugly in the life insurance business. In every case, it boiled down to one word: GREED.

The Knights of Columbus Insurance has allowed me to enjoy a career that has spanned some four decades with a company that's thrived in that highly focused market. Our company culture has and will always be focused on safety. We have never sold many of the products that got so many life insurance companies into trouble. Those products transferred the responsibility of correctly funding the vehicle from the company to the client. By design, we decided not to play in that end of the pool, and today we enjoy ratings that fewer than a handful of companies in the world have.

However, it's not simply about avoiding the land mines that clutter the financial services battlefield; it's also about building an organization that refuses to sit idly by and see our products or members attacked by those who seek to feather their own nests at the expense of the client.

In the late 1970s and early 1980s, replacement artists were cropping up on every corner advising clients to cancel their guaranteed products in lieu of higher interest rates they could enjoy on riskier investment products. As a result, entire companies disappeared from the financial services landscape as these scam artists traded short-term profits for their own personal gain.

Unfortunately, clients themselves paid the dearest price of all in these scenarios. The replacement artists said to naïve clients: "Give me an apple seed and we'll give you an orchard." Unsurprisingly, this didn't happen. Many of those agents and companies disappeared from the marketplace, leaving their clients high and dry.

TRAIN YOUR PEOPLE BETTER, AND YOU WILL GET BETTER RESULTS!

Our company made a major training commitment when this proliferation began. We decided that we would not allow any client to surrender a policy without having us personally visit their home to give them all of their options. We established what we call a "Conservation Department" and staffed it with top-notch professionals who were well versed in the consequences of making decisions to surrender their business.

Entire companies were shamefully teaching their agents how to mislead clients into thinking they were purchasing something that was going to return them double-digit returns. The returns disappeared as quickly as the agents churning out the business, causing Departments of Insurance in every state to issue new dictates demanding full disclosure.

Many unscrupulous agents migrated from company to company, tearing down client after client as they raped the investment and insurance landscape. These dishonest agents helped build many law firms with suits that addressed their lack of ethics.

Sadly, their trickery was actually encouraged by unscrupulous companies that encouraged agents to twist out older, guaranteed products in exchange for so-called high rates of return. The problem: They traded their guaranteed products for "pie-in-the-sky" returns that never materialized. The age of greed had been born and was blessed by the very companies that would have sworn off such practices only a decade earlier.

The 1987 movie *Wall Street* was a mirror of what would happened with the financial collapse of many great financial institutions as the new millennium was ushered in. Justice was as blind as the corporate bobbleheads who encouraged this greed and blessed those who took advantage of the poor consumer. Finally, "Justice" took off her mask and went after these thieves, and they made stealing illegal again, but not until a lot of damage was done.

It's little wonder that clients no longer trust anyone when it comes to taking this kind of advice today. What if every company selling financial products had made the prodigious effort to conserve lost business instead of actually rewarding their agents for twisting out the client's old reliable products for the new-fangled pie-in-the-sky promises? Unfortunately, they didn't—and that's why we have the mess we do today.

THE CAT WHO SAT ON THE HOT STOVE

A wronged customer is like the cat who sat on the hot stove. Because he got burned, he never sat there again. He decided not to sit on a cold stove either; he simply got out of the stove-sitting business. That's not a lot unlike how many clients feel today. They're no longer in the stove-sitting business. They only want guarantees, not promises.

When it's a part of your company's culture to aggressively defend your business, your competitor quickly learns that you won't take their claims lying down. I once wrote an article for the national publication *A.M. Best Magazine* entitled "When the Replacement Bug Stings, What Do You Do?" The entire premise of the article was that you must vigorously defend your product at all costs, regardless of whether you have a financial stake in the business.

If one of our customers decides that they want to sell their policy back to us because of some pie-in-the-sky deal, our client service philosophy is to uncompromisingly defend the quality of our business and forcefully require the replacing company to show cause and prove how their product is better.

This isn't meant to sound naïve. It goes without saying that no company can offer everything to everybody. If someone wants those higher risk products, we simply want to educate them as to what they are getting into and attempt to make them aware of the risks.

Did we always conserve every piece of business? Of course not; however, we currently enjoy an almost-100 percent persistency rating—one of the best in the industry. Rarely do we lose clients to less than honest companies, because we adamantly defend the business at all costs and demand face-to-face confrontations to anyone who wants to take it away. In short: We won't go down without a fight.

Are our agents financially rewarded for preserving a contract written decades ago by an agent who is long dead and gone? No, Are they given any credit or reward for doing the right thing for the client? No, but our very presence in the client's home or business to preserve and protect what they have built is all the evidence most of them need to ignore the demagoguery and preserve the business. After all, we've shown how important their buying decisions are to us by physically making ourselves a part of it.

We frequently not only come away preserving the business; we end up adding more. But shame on us for allowing our competition to get to our member client and establish a relationship in the first place. It's our job to be there to handle their needs and to protect their interests.

To that end, we want our agents to be in constant communication with their clients by mail, phone, or e-mail—at least on a monthly basis. Great automobile salesman Joe Girard once told me that he sent out 13,000 cards every month to his clients who had bought cars from him over the years. In January, he would wish them a "Happy New Year." In February, he would wish them a "Happy Valentine's Day." In March, he sent them "Happy St. Patrick's Day" greetings. In April, he would say "Happy IRS Day."

It really doesn't matter much *what* you say to them, as long as you're staying in touch and keeping yourself at the top of their minds. Girard said he even got "Change of Address" cards from his clients because they liked his cards so much and wanted to keep receiving them even after they had moved.

Do you stay in touch with your clients? One of my agents, Jim Spinelli—a terrific Million Dollar Round Table producer—sent a birthday card for seven consecutive years to a prospect who never bought a thing from him. After he sent the eighth birthday wish, the client called our office one day and asked to have Jim give him a ring. He was ready to buy.

Never once during the span of those eight years did his other agent send a card, a holiday greeting, or even a thank you note—even though he had purchased a $5 million permanent policy from them. By staying in touch, Jim was able to capture a client for life—one who purchased much from Jim over the years. Staying in touch pays big dividends. If they're not a client yet, be patient; they soon will be!

TAKEAWAY SERVICING AND SELLING TACTICS

1. When a client is approached by your competitor, train the client to give them your card and tell them that you do the buying for them. Protect their interests above all else.
2. Stay in touch with your clients as often as it takes to have a strong presence of mind with them.

CHAPTER 23

MENTOR YOUR CLIENT

*What does mentoring a client have
to do with anything? You say nothing?
I say everything!*

Mentors and coaches have to love you enough to give you not only the good news but also the bad news. Fabulous companies like Milliken and Disney got that way because of their undying commitment to coaching and mentoring their people to greatness. Great mentors emphasize the learning process. They are great teachers first and great coaches second.

Great coaches and mentors never miss a training opportunity. They see both failure and success as power forums to teach their players how to get it right. They utilize prevailing lessons about character, courage, and honor to make compelling points. In doing so, they make a lasting impression on those whom they mentor and coach.

Superb mentoring relies on superb storytelling. People learn best from examples that are applied to real-life stories about situations to which they can relate. The unforgettable insight they glean from this process helps develop empathy and understanding of others' challenges and goals. Quality coaching can help a customer service representative become "client cozy."

GOOD MENTORS HAVE A NUMBER OF ENDEARING QUALITIES:

1. They have an **honest desire to help**, to give something back to the profession of which they are a part.

2. The **success and positive experiences** they've had in their lives make them great candidates for showing others the way.

3. They **make the time** and **have the energy** to legitimately help others to achieve greatness. If your mentor is short-tempered or impatient, find a new one.

4. They constantly **stay in school** and remain up to date on the latest and greatest information available to them. They spend an inordinate amount of time studying and staying up to date. Since they're always teaching others, they're always learning themselves.

5. Finally, and most importantly, they have **mastered effective communication skills** to "sell" their message to others. They evolve more as counselors, advocates, and facilitators who maximize their networking skills to get the absolute most from their relationships with others.

The life insurance industry's Million Dollar Round Table group has developed a terrific mentoring program. As someone who has been an MDRT member and has addressed the main platform of MDRT, it's been an honor to be exposed to these great mentors. They see themselves as leaders, but they don't throw their weight around. On the contrary, many are as humble and as low-key as anyone you'll ever meet. They see their assignment as a responsibility to not only others but to their profession and to themselves.

What does all of this have to do with developing great customer service representatives? Absolutely everything! Great mentoring is about counseling, guidance, and encouragement.

Not only do candidates and mentees grow significantly from this relationship; mentors themselves blossom into better people. Study after study shows that both the mentor's and the mentee's business grow significantly from this connection.

THE SWEET TITLE OF COACH

I have had the privilege of doing play-by-play for football and baseball at the high school level over the years, both from the press box and on radio in Lexington, South Carolina, and St. Cloud, Florida as well as Pop Warner football at Harmony, Florida.

When my children were growing up, I had the privilege of coaching at the Pop Warner level. Occasionally, someone will come up to me at church or in a restaurant and say "Hi, Coach." I know I am speaking to one of the kids with whom I used to work.

For anyone who has ever coached youngsters, that is the kindest title anyone could call you. It is a show of respect to accord you the title, despite not having done it for years.

Coaches are a special breed of people. They spend more time with children than the parents of those kids do. It is quite understandable that they would bond with them as I did with my own coach and mentor, the late J.W. Ingram. A love-hate relationship evolves as kids try to please their coach with good playmaking and victories.

My youngest son, Christopher, was an All-Conference center and a pretty decent athlete. His older twin brothers, Cory and Jason, were (as they say in the movie *Rudy*) five-foot-nothing and a hundred-nothing.

In four years at St. Cloud High School, my sons never missed a football practice. In four years, they never started and about the only time they ever got into a game was when the St. Cloud Bulldogs were well ahead or well behind. In four years, no matter what level on which they played, their teams never lost to archrival Osceola in nearby Kissimmee.

They never missed a practice, a game, or a class in school, receiving perfect attendance honors. Did they ever want to quit? If they did, they never shared that with their parents. Were they hurt by their lack of playing time? If they were, they never told us or their coaches. They simply showed up as if they were starting every play on both sides of the ball. I always admired that in my sons.

Recently I came across a letter that was written to them by their high school football coach, John Wallauer, who is now retired. Here is the letter.

Dear Cory and Jason,

I will address this letter to both of you because, as you well know, in four years I could never tell you apart anyway. I hope you never took this personally. During my 25 years coaching career, I have worked with at least six pairs of twins and I could not tell them apart either.

From time to time, I sit down at the end of the year to write a letter such as this one to some of the young men who have been a part of my program. This is the only letter I have written this year.

I want to thank you for all that you have done for St. Cloud High School and my football program. What did Cory and Jason do for the St. Cloud High football program? Did you set records? Catch touchdown passes? No. You contributed something more important. You gave our program "character."

Your courage, work ethic, honesty and integrity set an example for others to follow. There were times when you could have given up and quit, but you did not. You simply accepted the challenge and worked harder.

This letter is about "respect." Respect is what you have worked so hard to earn and so rightfully deserve. As the years pass and the memories fade, as they have over the past 25 years, I know I will remember at least two things: the win in the "Spurs" (St. Cloud's only win in 50 years in that stadium) and the "Aun-sters!"

In closing, I would like to share one last thought with you. Do not ever forget that your success is the result of the love and guidance given you by your parents. Young people are the product of their environment and your environment, no doubt, was a special one. I know they are proud of you; I hope you are as proud of them.

Best of luck always, Cory and Jason. I hope your life is filled with happiness and success.

Sincerely,

Coach John Wallauer

P.S. Please do not be offended when we meet and I ask, "Which one are you?"

GREAT MENTORS ENVISION SUCCESS IN OTHERS

The late Coach Carl Stegall came to my hometown of Lexington, South Carolina, with a former neighbor of mine, Coach Bob Whitehead, to take over the basketball fortunes at Lexington High School. Stegall had been a successful coach in the upper state of South Carolina.

Stegall's peers immediately questioned him: "Why Lexington? All they know is football and baseball!" Stegall's response was simple: "If they have great football players, then they are bound to have great basketball players, too. A great athlete is a great athlete."

Stegall and Whitehead helped Lexington turn their round ball fortunes around, but it was not easy. But then, nothing ever came easy for the lanky Newberry College graduate.

Carl Stegall grew up in the Anderson County, South Carolina "backwoods," as it was known in those days. There were only a dozen boys at Anderson's Melton High School, located between Pendleton and Slabtown. Stegall got five of his buddies together and approached the school about forming a basketball team.

They laughed at him. "You barely have enough kids to fill a roster," they said.

"We have six," said Stegall. "All we need is five to field a team." They chuckled, "What about fouls?" His response: "We can't afford to have many."

Those six brave youngsters, led by the lanky Stegall, clawed their way to the state championship in their first year, a real life *Hoosiers* story.

The remarkable accomplishment didn't go unnoticed. Newberry College learned of Stegall's talents and recruited him to play ball. He went on to star for the Indians in the late 1940s and early 50s. In 1950, he was named to the South Carolina All-State basketball team.

After college, Stegall followed his passion for sports and teaching. He became a teacher, coach, and athletic director in Greenville, Columbia, Lexington, and Anderson schools, a career that spanned more than 39 years.

He was the co-founder of the South Carolina State Basketball Coaches Association and was an inductee into the Brooklyn-Cayce

High School Basketball Hall of Fame. He was also installed into the Newberry College Hall of Fame. This is what great mentors do—they give back to their profession.

Carl Stegall touched many people's lives over the years. All you have to do is look at me and you know I never played basketball for him. I'm about as wide as I am tall, but what I lack in height I make up for with slowness, which accounts for the reason I never made it past the intramural level of basketball at Lexington, that is, I'm short but I'm slow.

Stegall coached me in track and in football. No, I was not a sprinter on the track team. My head football and baseball, Coach J.W. Ingram, used to accuse me of running in one place too long. Stegall did use me as a shot put and discus guy on the track team. He also coached the B football team, which is where I encountered him.

I recall it was a nice May afternoon when Coach Stegall came to the door of Jim Shirley's algebra class to ask if he could speak to me. Mr. Shirley and I had an understanding. If I did not snore too loud, he would not toss me out on my heels. He knew I would never be a NASA rocket scientist, but he also knew I needed algebra to graduate. So we cut a deal.

Satisfied that I had already napped long enough and anxious to put a stop to my snoring, Mr. Shirley readily agreed to allow me a "leave of absence" from his class. In the hall, Coach Stegall asked if I wanted to be a kicker. "Kick what?" I asked incredulously. "A football!" he exclaimed.

Are you kidding me? I had trouble walking and chewing gum at the same time. But I gave it a go, and not only did it get me out of Coach E.T. "Charge" Driggers dreaded head-on exercises, but it also allowed me to have what little notoriety I would enjoy in my otherwise mediocre athletic career. In fact, it earned me an All-State Shrine Bowl nomination during my senior year, though a broken leg put a stop to my athletic career.

ENVISION SUCCESS! KEEP YOUR HEAD DOWN AND FOLLOW THROUGH!

"You have to see the ball through the goal post," explained Stegall. "Envision success. Hold your arms out in front of you and create an imaginary goal post. When you approach the ball, keep your head down, kick the ball squarely, and follow through by bringing your kicking leg straight through the imaginary goal post. After you kick the ball, reach down and grab a blade of grass. The crowd will let you know if the ball went through the uprights." Though it differs from one sport to another, a lot of coaches have one piece of advice that they offer to players: "Keep your head down and follow through." It's an interesting philosophy that, fascinatingly enough, works in real life, too. Many athletes also find that the crowd will let you know whether or not they approve of your plays—and the same is true with your customers and clients. They vote with their wallets and their loyalty to you and your company. Do your best to keep them as raving fans.

WINNING ISN'T FINAL; LOSING ISN'T FATAL

My mentor was a man named Coach James Wyman Ingram, who passed away at the ripe old age of 94. To fully appreciate his impact on the community of Lexington, South Carolina, you had to be one of the thousands of people he coached and taught in his four decades on the gridirons, diamonds, and hardwoods, as well as in the classrooms of Lexington.

In some cases, he actually coached or taught as many as three generations in one family. He coached many of my immediate family members as well as my uncles, Arthur and Eli Mack. He coached the late Congressman Floyd Spence, who not only earned a Shrine Bowl nomination, but also a full scholarship to the University of South Carolina.

On February 18, 1984, I had the privilege of heading up an Ingram-Driggers Appreciation Day Banquet thanking and honoring both Ingram and his longtime sidekick, E.T. "Charge" Driggers. One of Ingram's "boys," as he liked to call them, Congressman Spence, could not be there that night.

He wrote in a letter to the gathering that evening that no one other than his parents had had a greater impact on his life than Coach Ingram. "I might not be where I am today were it not for Coach Ingram. He was solely responsible for my appearance in the Shrine Bowl and me getting a scholarship to the University of South Carolina."

Both led to Spence earning a law degree and later entering the field of politics. He wasn't the only political prodigy of Ingram's. Others included former Lexington Mayors Hugh Rogers and Eli Mack Jr., as well as a variety of school board members, state representatives, and other political officials.

But that wasn't Ingram's greatest contribution. One could make the argument that his own accomplishments as a four-sport letterman at Newberry College were dwarfed only by his awesome record as a coach for nearly four decades at Lexington. His efforts at Newberry earned him membership into the Newberry College Hall of Fame in 1989.

In 1987, he was the very first inductee into the Lexington High School Hall of Fame. In 1993, the South Carolina Coaches Association enshrined him into their Coaches Hall of Fame.

On November 24, 2001, Coach Ingram was inducted into the Alabama Sports Hall of Fame for Dekalb County, the community where he scored the first ever touchdown for the school's newly formed football team in 1926.

His Wildcat teams amassed a 218-77-10 record on the gridiron, including three state championships. His baseball teams earned one state title and 16 conference championships while amassing a 111-41 record. In addition, he coached boys' and girls' basketball to a 174-75 record, as well as coaching track and teaching Phys Ed.

At one time, he was the most successful active football coach in the state of South Carolina and among the top ten in the nation. He coached every sport at Lexington, drove the bus, and even acted as the janitor. In his day, you did it all. In addition, he served as athletic director.

In 1949, he coached the very first Horse Bowl in Camden, South Carolina. In 1954, Coach Ingram was selected to coach the Sandlappers in the annual Shrine Bowl. His squad was a prodigious underdog to the larger, faster North Carolina Tar Heel team. In fact, he had only one player over 200 pounds on the entire squad. South Carolina recorded the greatest upset in the history of the Shrine Bowl by a 27-7 score on the shoulders of 165-pound King Dixon of Laurens. The biggest reward for Coach Ingram was the inscription on the wall of the Shriners Children's Hospital: "Strong legs run so weak legs may walk."

Ingram's football teams were known for their unique offensive alignments and unusual blocking schemes. While serving in the U.S. Navy during World War II, he met the legendary Paul Brown of the Cleveland Browns. When he returned to South Carolina, he brought back a blocking scheme never heard of in high school athletics at that time, a concept called *cross-blocking*.

Floyd Spence asked his college coaches at the University of South Carolina about cross-blocking. "We don't do that in college," explained the coaches. "That's something they do in the pros."

Ingram's stingy defenses were usually outmanned and outweighed. What made him so remarkable is that he took very ordinary kids from a very ordinary community and taught them how to play in an extraordinary way.

Almost every high school in America today platoons players. When you played for Ingram, you played four quarters and most kids played every down, which made what he accomplished at Lexington so remarkable. He won over 70 percent of his contests. His offensive football teams averaged over 300 yards per game and his defenses yielded less than 100 yards every outing.

Executive Sports Editor Herman Helms of Columbia's *State Newspaper*, speaking about Ingram at the 1984 banquet attended by over 1,000 fans and supporters, said Ingram looked more like a college professor than a football coach.

"He was as organized as any coach I've ever seen," said Helms. "His special teams were ahead of their time. I once asked him about the success of the special teams, and he remarked sensibly that on most kicking plays, all the players start out unblocked and open. Why not take advantage of it?"

Former Saluda and Lower Richland football coach Mooney Player called him the greatest offensive mind he had ever met—high school, college, or pros.

Former Swansea coach Doug Bennett called him a gentleman. "In all the years I knew Coach Ingram," said Bennett, "he never said a word about his faith but I knew he was a God-fearing man."

"I first learned of him when my high school football team in York (near Rock Hill) was playing Lexington," said Bennett. "One of the kids on our team broke his leg against Lexington. Not even a week went by when we received a check in the mail representing money that Coach Ingram and the people of Lexington had raised for the young man. He had lots of class."

Former Presbyterian College coach Cally Gault, another of the speakers at the 1984 banquet, called Ingram one of the most gracious men he had ever met in athletics.

"It must be a wonderful thing to take a thin pine board and a bit of string and some glue and to make of it a violin that would solve out the great 'Ave Maria'," said Gault. "And it must be a beautiful thing to take a bit of gold and a few springs and to make of it a timepiece that would keep pace with the magnificent sun. And it must be a gorgeous thing to take a canvas and a bit of paint and a brush and to make of it a painting such as the *Malaise Angelis*. It is a splendid thing to take a boy, to discipline him, coach him, and make of him a man. That's what Coach J.W. Ingram did with so many young men and women for nearly four decades."

Despite all the remarkable things Ingram did in both the classroom as an English and French teacher and in the athletic arena, he was a husband to two great women in his life, Christine B. (first wife) and Ethelyn J. (second wife), succeeding each of them.

Clearly, he was a surrogate father to me and many others. One touching story resounds even today about a young man named Tillman Craft, who came to Lexington from the Edmund community. He was a product of a broken home, causing him to be separated from his seven brothers and sisters in the fifth grade. Coach Ingram learned of the young man's plight and became his surrogate father.

Unable to put him up in his own small home because of small children of his own, Coach Ingram quietly let the boy move into the old Lexington gym that stood some two blocks from his home on North Lake Drive in Lexington. He fed and clothed Tillman, never asking for assistance or permission.

In return, Tillman slept at night in the gym at night, bathed in the showers there, and kept the floors cleaned as his rent. Coach and Mrs. Ingram kept him in clean clothes and saw to his medical and physical needs.

Soon the authorities found out about it and forced Coach Ingram to move the young man out of the gym. They found him a room over a doctor's office near Coach Ingram's home. Coach continued to feed and provide for Tillman.

After high school, he enrolled at the University of South Carolina, where he studied law enforcement. He graduated with honors from USC—the first in his family to go to college. He entered the U.S. Army, where he served his country and also excelled as an athlete.

Tillman entered the military and was a multiple sport standout in the armed forces. After completing his military duty, Tillman returned to South Carolina where he entered the University of South Carolina Law School, earning a juris doctorate.

He later went to work for the FBI where he built a remarkable career as one of J. Edgar Hoover's finest. After retiring from the FBI, he opened his own security agency in Houston, Texas, that named among its clients the Houston Rockets and the Houston Astros. He later retired a second time and bought an oil company.

You have to ask yourself the question: Which side of the law would a homeless fifth grade child have ended up on were it not for the love and concern of James Wymon Ingram?

Indeed, he was more than a humble teacher and football coach. He was an icon, a mentor, an advocate, and a great teacher, all of which made him a great coach.

TAKEAWAY SERVICING AND SELLING TACTICS

1. Become an advocate for your customer. Clients want you in their corner.
2. Mentor your customer service representative employee so they can properly mentor the client. They can't give away that which they don't own.
3. Define and envision what success means to the customer so that they will come away from their relationship with you and your company as YOUR advocate.

CHAPTER 24

CUSTOMER-DRIVEN LEADERSHIP IS ABOUT ADVOCACY AND MENTORING

Great customer-driven leadership is about advocacy, caring, and loving the customer.

While traveling in Europe in April 1986, my wife and I found ourselves right in the middle of the conflict between the United States and Libya. We had just entered what used to be West Germany when a suspected Libyan terrorist blew up a pub, killing several Americans. Several days later, just as we were arriving in France, the United States responded by strategically bombing Libya.

While we were in France, I listened as 80 percent of the European world criticized then-President Reagan for the retaliation. It occurred to me that the price of Mr. Reagan's leadership must have truly been loneliness.

As we flew on to England, the criticism had grown, and was aimed this time at Prime Minister Margaret Thatcher. According to the Gallup Poll taken that day, 65 percent of her own people leveled some of the harshest criticism on her administration for allowing the American bombers to fly from England's shores.

The French, who refused our request for help, were praised for their so-called restraint. Mrs. Thatcher—a gutsy woman who made a gutsy decision—was rebuffed instead of praised by her own people.

In both cases, responsible leaders made courageous decisions in what they perceived were the best interests of their people. Neither won the popularity contest; yet given the opportunity to decide again, I'd imagine that both would probably make the same decision today.

Sometimes we have to take on the role of courageous guides in our roles as customer care representatives and make similar spirited decisions to exceed the client's expectations. And just as it was with President Reagan and Prime Minister Thatcher, these decisions won't always make us the most popular leaders. However, as long as they are made with the best intentions, they will likely lead to constructive results.

SOME COMMON MISCONCEPTIONS ABOUT CUSTOMER-DRIVEN LEADERSHIP

There are two major misconceptions in North America today concerning leadership, the first of which is the confusion of leadership with management. The two are not the same. Leadership is a deeply rooted philosophy, whereas management is the appropriation of certain skills to complete the tasks one faces.

And with the flattening of the leadership matrix in corporations all over the world today, more gallant decisions are being made from further down the food chain; that is, there is really not much middle management anymore.

The second misconception is that people are born with the skills necessary to succeed in life. Not so; skills are developed and learned. Leadership is all about developing those skills to their maximum level of efficiency in an organization and then allowing customer service folks to adopt that role. As a student who has researched habits of prominent leaders, I have concluded that these people have a number of things in common. Whether by design or accident, it matters not.

Whether you are in sales or management or both, one of the most important characteristics for you to possess is good leadership skills.

I've learned two incontrovertible facts about leadership in my nearly four decades in the insurance business and on the platform:

1. The price of leadership is loneliness.
2. When leading, you can't be concerned with what other people think about you.

Successful leaders, both great and ruthless, have a number of identifiable characteristics. Here are a few that customer service people also need to have to be better at everything they do.

1. GREAT CUSTOMER-DRIVEN LEADERS GAZE INTO LIFE'S CRYSTAL BALL.

Remarkable leaders have developed a vision for the future that is founded on a sound set of personal goals and business principles. They know where they're headed in life; and more often than not, that direction is clearly marked in a written format that includes several key ingredients.

First, they know how they want to feel after the game is over. They have the capacity to imagine themselves in "victory lane." Second, they've specifically defined their objectives. If they wish to lose weight, for example, they know specifically how much they want to knock off and how they're going to do it. If they want to increase their wealth, they know exactly what they desire to have, and the strategies they're going to use to attain it.

Third, they place deadlines on themselves. In short, they make a contract with themselves and they abide by cutoff dates. Fourth, they clearly define the obstacles that they believe might stand in the way of the goal. Knowing what to overcome is half the battle.

Fifth, they hop in and *just do it*. They adjust from failure and try again until they reach their objective; not by trial and error, but rather by trial and success.

2. GREAT CUSTOMER-DRIVEN LEADERS ARE DECISIVE.

The biggest problem facing today's leaders is their reluctance to make decisions. The old expression "ready, fire, aim" might best describe the philosophy among today's current leadership success stories; in other words, they make decisions and then live with the consequences. They're risk takers and boardroom riverboat gamblers determined to get the most from their company and their product. They are well aware of the fact that *indecision* is, in fact, *decision*. They don't want critical decisions being left to fate, time, circumstances, or default. They want the right to decide, even if they fail.

3. GREAT CUSTOMER-DRIVEN LEADERS LOVE TO FAIL.

Productive leaders understand that failure is the process by which we succeed. They know that a certain number of failures must accompany every success. For example, the baseball player who's hitting .333 is failing two out of every three times he travels to the plate. He earns over a million bucks a year. Yet the guy who's hitting .250 earns only a fraction of that.

The difference between them is only one more hit in every 20 times at bat! As management guru Tom Peters has said: People have got to learn to fail faster in order to keep up in the changing business world.

4. GREAT CUSTOMER-DRIVEN LEADERS AREN'T CONCERNED ABOUT WHAT OTHERS THINK ABOUT THEM.

If leadership boiled down to someone taking a poll and deciding on what the majority thought at that very instant in time, then Mr. Gallup would be our president. Successful leaders don't make decisions based on what's going to make them popular. They analyze the situation and decide what's in the best interest of the majority concerned. Many times, that decision can make them very lonely and unpopular. However, leadership should not be a popularity contest. The most popular student isn't always the most likely to succeed.

5. GREAT CUSTOMER-DRIVEN LEADERS SUBSCRIBE TO A SET OF STANDARDS, VALUES, AND DISCIPLINES FROM WHICH THEY WILL NOT VEER.

One of the truly great hallmarks of Ronald Reagan's presidency is the fact that, like him or not, you never had to question where he stood on an issue. He never once vacillated on important matters; he made his opinion known, and he stuck with his convictions. While values and discipline are not the only factors affecting success in life, they play a truly important part. If they were, only the football teams with the highest ethical standards and conduct would succeed. When asked whether discipline and character were keys to winning football games, the great coach and philosopher Bobby Bowden once said, "If they were, Army and Navy would be playing for the National Championship every year." The Knights of Columbus are another example of a company that has high ratings and its certification because it nevers offer bait-and-switch products that transfer the mantle of responsibility from the company to the clients.

Values and discipline aren't the only things that matter, but they are a major piece in the puzzle.

6. GREAT CUSTOMER-DRIVEN LEADERS ARE HONEST.

There used to be a time when the word *honest* was considered sort of corny. Fairness and justice were never the issue, only profit. However, today's great leaders have found that the two go hand in hand—that it indeed takes *honesty* to be *profitable*.

When some *crazy* person poisoned an untold number of Tylenol bottles with cyanide in the early 1980s, Johnson & Johnson didn't say, "It's not our fault." Instead, they faced the issue head on—an approach that, to this day, stands out as one of the great corporate leadership decisions of our time. Their concern for their customers' health and safety was so great that they were willing to take a short-term $100 million-plus loss for the benefit of staying atop the world's corporate leadership. It was, in fact, the right thing to do for all the right reasons. Johnson & Johnson has rebounded nicely, proving again why it's in fact one of the great corporations in the world today.

7. GREAT CUSTOMER-DRIVEN LEADERS EXPECT A LOT FROM THEIR PEOPLE.

If you expect a lot you'll get a lot. Expect little, and you may get even less. And you must "inspect" what you "expect." You get the behavior you measure and monitor. Show me the reward system of an institution and I'll show you where they place their values. Similarly, good leaders never expect their people to do something that they themselves would not do. If one's philosophy is sound, then there's never a question about the decision. That is best reflected in the attitude and actions of the leader.

8. GREAT CUSTOMER-DRIVEN LEADERS LISTEN AND LEARN TO LOVE OTHERS.

When your people are crying out to be heard, they do so both directly and indirectly by crying out "notice me!" and "love me!" So show them some affection, and learn to pay attention. Reward them for a job well done. Admonish them when their behavior warrants correction. Great leaders sense the need to build others up, many times even at their own expense. This is the reason they always deal with the performance and never the performer. They know that they need to love the person, regardless of the person's behavior. If their behavior is unsuitable, then speak to that; but never the quality of the performer him- or herself. You must always separate the two. It's okay to hate the performance, but not the performer.

9. GREAT CUSTOMER-DRIVEN LEADERS ACCEPT RESPONSIBILITY.

They keenly seek the role of leadership because it carries with it the awesome burden of responsibility. They are not drawn to power, nor do they shrink from it. They see it as an incidental by-product of the leadership role. They always hold themselves accountable and never blame outside factors, like interest rates or the stock market. They understand that if they fall behind in the marketplace, it's not the market that failed you; it's simply reflecting your latest performance rating.

10. GREAT CUSTOMER-DRIVEN LEADERS EMBRACE IN A CONSTANT STATE OF CHANGE AND ARE AMAZINGLY FLEXIBLE.

The trouble with the future is it ain't what it used to be! Great leaders realize this and are constantly innovating because of it. This forces them to look at old problems with new solutions. They view "state of the art" as state of necessity. They spend thousands of dollars on training and working with their people. They adopt the philosophy that "you can't have rabbit stew until you catch the rabbit"; in other words, you can't dispense information that you don't have.

The stock market has fluctuated over the years; those factors brought the best out of many of the great performers. Fate dealt them a severe blow. Many lost a fortune on a Monday, but began to rebuild on a Tuesday. Great leaders possess flexibility and resiliency. They bend but never break. They give, but never completely.

11. GREAT CUSTOMER-DRIVEN LEADERS HAVE A CHARMING SENSE OF HUMOR.

They laugh at their failures and take their successes in stride. They constantly have fun, finding genuine lightheartedness in seemingly humorless situations. They see the comedy of their shortcomings and accept them as part of their nature and personality. They possess an enthusiasm for life that transcends any problems they face.

12. GREAT CUSTOMER-DRIVEN LEADERS ARE COMMITTED.

Quite simply, they persist in their cause with reckless abandon. First, they believe in what they are doing. Second, the word "quit" simply doesn't exist in their vocabulary. Third, they have powerfully strong convictions about their cause, seeing that cause as part of a bigger picture. Fourth, they are self-disciplined beyond what most people can understand. Fifth, they are uncomplicated and hang tough through good and bad. Sixth, they understand sacrifice. Seventh, they enjoy the process of work. Eighth, they have morals that they refuse to compromise. Ninth, they subscribe to the theory "If it is to be, it's up to me." They know that the buck stops with them.

TAKEAWAY SERVICING AND SELLING TACTICS

1. Customer-driven leadership is about advocacy, counseling, and caring for the customer.
2. Other qualities include being decisive and committed, learning from failure, displaying honesty, and constantly learning from and teaching others.

CHAPTER 25

THE OLD WAY IS RARELY THE BEST WAY BECAUSE CHANGE IS CONSTANT

The customer will let you know.

THROW OUT THE OLD WAY!

If you have "always" done it the old way, then there's a very good chance that the old way simply isn't working anymore. That is a fact with which many organizations are coming to grips today. It begs the question: Why does it take so long for us to recognize the obvious?

Did you know that the 10 most in-demand jobs this year weren't even around five years ago? We're preparing kids for jobs that don't yet exist, using technology that is yet to be invented to solve problems we do not even have. Good customer service means knowing where you want to be after those cards have been dealt.

When customers are unhappy, it is because we did not solve their problems—pure and simple. Our number-one job—whether it is delivering the right pizza on time or delivering a speech to an audience of 1,000—is to solve the consumer's problem or meet a particular need.

IT APPLIES TO EVERY ASPECT OF LIFE TODAY

Even educational institutions are facing similar customer service issues today. With so many people unemployed or underemployed, many are returning to the classroom to reload and gather new skill sets that will allow them to be more marketable in an ever-competitive world.

The net result is that it is putting enormous pressure on colleges and universities everywhere, but most especially in the junior college ranks where enrollment has skyrocketed to 125 percent or more in most institutions.

I recently gave a speech to a software consortium of community colleges whose enrollments have rocketed to 125 percent of their projections. Conversely, their budgets have been slashed to 90 to 95 percent of their previous levels. They can't even build classrooms fast enough to accommodate the skyrocketing demand for new classes. Why? Record layoffs are driving people back into the classroom to look for new disciplines to help them reenter the job market.

The challenge for many of these community colleges is their enrollments have increased but their budgets have not, leaving them with the challenge of delivering quality education at community college rates. The student-customer is not a happy camper in many of these institutions.

The students want more skills and they will acquire them in the least expensive fashion possible. For most of these unhappy customers, that means to trot down to the local community college and scarf up some courses that will make them immediately competitive in today's marketplace.

Many of these courses, quite frankly, are obsolete before the ink is dry in the textbook. By the time the instructors get the material out of their mouths, the information is already old.

Case in point, if you or your kid is in a two-year technical school, the knowledge that he or she would gain in year one would be completely obsolete by the time that student graduates. More than ever, continuing education is the hallmark of real growth. Knowledge, like bananas and tomatoes, has a short shelf life. This is why an organization like Toastmasters is so important.

Toastmasters is a forum that gives people a place to hone their skill set and develop their communication and leadership skills, which is quite often the single difference between them and the person with whom they are competing for the job.

I joined a Toastmasters Club in Cayce, South Carolina, in 1974 because a client of mine, Patrick Callahan, extorted me. He was about to purchase a very substantial life insurance policy from my company, the Knights of Columbus Insurance.

Patrick was a lector at St. Peter's Catholic Church in Columbia, South Carolina. He felt that if I joined Toastmasters it would help me in my own lector skills. I thought Toastmasters was a bunch of old fogies who sat around toasting one another and wanted nothing to do with it, and I as much as told him so.

Patrick suggested that he could shop his very substantial insurance policy with other companies. My response was quick and simple: When do we meet? It was the single greatest thing I have ever done to advance my career.

To this very day, when I'm in town, I still go to Toastmasters every week of my life I belong to Osceola Toastmasters Club 1841 in Kissimmee, Florida. We meet every Friday morning at 7:30 AM. It has been the single most powerful ingredient in the advancement of my career.

Go to www.Toastmasters.Org and enter your zip code. A list of every Toastmasters Club in your general area will pop up, showing locations and times at which they meet.

DON'T WORRY ABOUT WHAT YOU ARE GOING TO BE WHEN YOU GROW UP; IT HASN'T BEEN INVENTED YET!

Because of the constantly changing times, my favorite mantra to my three sons when they were growing up was "Do not worry about what you are going to be when you grow up; it hasn't been invented yet."

According to the U.S. Department of Labor, today's college graduates will have 10 to 14 jobs by the time they reach age 38. One in four workers has been with their current employer for less than a year. One in two has been there for less than five years.

Did you know that myspace.com subscribers totaled over 200 million last year alone? If myspace.com were a country, it would be the fifth largest in the world between Indonesia and Brazil. And MySpace is but one of hundreds of social media sites that have blossomed into existence, soaking up what seems to be an insatiable need for today's customers to communicate differently— be it via Facebook, Twitter, or whatever the latest and greatest forum may be.

In 2006, there were 2 billion hits on Google. In 2007, that number skyrocketed to 31 billion. Today there are over 50 billion per year. So what happened "B.G." (Before Google)? How did we get answers to important questions? How did we get the information we needed at a moment's notice? And how does this apply to your business? Because unhappy customers are driving people to other venues to seek their information. It is so critically important to keep your customer happy— because they have plenty of ways nowadays of finding another vendor who will in a heartbeat.

The first text message was sent in December of 1992. Today, the total number of text messages in the next 24 hours easily exceeds the entire population of the entire planet. It took radio 38 years to reach 50 million people. It took television 13 years. It took the Internet just four years. It took iPod three years. Facebook did it in two years. Twitter got there in six months. In 1984, there were a thousand Internet devices on the planet. In 1992, that zoomed to a million. Today, there are easily over a trillion.

By 2013, super computers will exceed the computation capabilities of the human brain. By 2049, the equivalent of a $1,000-computer (today's value) will exceed the capabilities of the entire human species.

What is driving all of this demand? Answer: Unhappy customers who are seeking answers elsewhere. Make no mistake, when a customer is unhappy they will scream it from the mountaintop—and today's technology supplies them with countless avenues by which they can do so. Oh, yes, they will advise others, but the most telling way they address the issue is to simply take their business elsewhere—and bring their friends, family, and anyone who will listen with them.

SUPPLY VERSUS DEMAND AND DIMINISHING

In the next hour, 67 babies will be born in the United States, 274 in China, and 375 in India. Scientist Edward O. Wilson once said, "The key problem facing humanity in the coming century is how to bring a better quality of life—for 8 billion or more people—without wrecking the environment entirely in the attempt."

This global village of which we are a part is clearly marked by trends that are constantly shaping how we deal with the needs of our consuming public. With the proliferation of options driven by the Internet, unhappy people will no longer tolerate simply "adequate" service. They will begin to demand excellence.

Does that mean that people have abandoned face-to-face contact with others? It is tough to court over the Internet. How can you possibly develop human relationships without face-to-face contact?

I conduct 52 online meetings per year with the field agents across the state of Florida who work for our insurance agency. Do these meetings take the place of a good, strong sales seminar? Absolutely not; however, they do save the agents the trouble of traveling for up to half of their business day to attend an educational session that they can attend in their pajamas from the comfort of their home office. We still meet with our agency staff monthly, but those meetings are now designed to take them to a higher level in their training.

Today's customers will get their needs met one way or the other. My failure to equip my agents with the latest in knowledge and skills will hasten their demise as an agent or their departure to another company who will provide them with those needs. Because my agents are my internal customers, the way in which I educate and train them will dictate how they educate and motivate their clients—not only to buy life insurance, annuities, and long term care, but to serve their ongoing needs. When unhappy customers go elsewhere to get their needs met, they have effectively "fired you" on the spot.

Charles Kettering, the grand old man of General Motors who held over 300 patents, once said, "If you have always done it that way, it is probably wrong." I wonder what Mr. Kettering would think about the way the automobile industry has failed to keep up with change. He's got to be doing flips in his grave! At one time in history, there were a couple of thousand automobile companies. Did that make the automobile a bad idea? No. It was a bad idea for 2,000 of them to be building them. Now that we are down to the chosen few players who remain in the business, it begs the question: "How can they improve on what they deliver to their customer?" In the end, the customer fires the company when it fails to deliver.

It's the customer's opinion of the bad news, stupid, and it travels faster today than ever before.

TAKEAWAY SERVICING AND SELLING TACTICS
1. If it ain't broke, break it.
2. If it is broke, fix it.
3. The old way is rarely the best way because change is constant.
4. Customers have more ways than ever to find new products/ services, and new ways to complain about yours.

CHAPTER 26

RESPOND TO THE CLIENT EVEN IF YOU CANNOT PROVIDE AN IMMEDIATE SOLUTION

Find a way to be different.

Jiddo, my grandfather, taught me many different values. One of his favorite expressions was "Hiyetti, find out what the poor people are doing . . . then don't do it."

"What do you mean?" I asked. "Find out what the successful folks do and emulate them." Good sage advice from an uneducated immigrant.

His advice has carried over into all aspects of my life today. I think differently because that was how my mentor taught me to think. He began that teaching process with me as early as I can remember. I recall bagging groceries in his grocery store at the age of five. I was not yet even in school. He taught me about a work ethic. We all worked from early ages because that was the belief system in our family.

We never believed in allowances because we were too poor to have them. Consequently, I never gave my children allowances, either. In fact, I went totally in the opposite direction. I actually charged my children for living in my home. The allowances in our home worked like this: "If there is enough food left over, you get to eat. If there is an empty bed, you get to sleep."

I actually charged my children $228 per month to live in my home. They had to pay their life insurance (I sold them the policy). They had to set some money aside for their college education and they had to give a little back to God (that's how we did it in our house).

We started them with checking accounts when they were six years old. When Quicken came along, they learned how to manage their money on a computer. I would challenge them to invest their money. In fact, if they got over $500 in their checking account and they did not invest it, I threatened to confiscate it.

Christopher, my youngest son, looked up the word confiscate and nearly went ballistic. "Dad, you aren't taking my money," he exclaimed. "I will if you don't invest it. Just think of me as the government. I'm like a black hole. Once your money goes to me, it's gone forever."

PERCEPTION IS REALITY

When I was growing up, I had a simple perception about life: You had to work hard to be successful. The money I earned working at my grandfather's grocery store was turned over to my mom and dad to help run the home. When I got older, I began working at a service station for my Little League baseball coach, Ralph Corley.

I earned a dollar an hour changing tires and pumping gas and would sometimes work 80 to 90 hours a week during the summer. I turned all the money over to my parents to help feed my 10 brothers and sisters. All of the children in our home worked and we all kicked in financially to help feed the family.

In high school, I worked at the service station and helped my uncles in the family grocery store, which they took over upon the death of my grandfather, Eli Mack, Sr. I also wrote for three newspapers part time and drove a school bus, which surprisingly paid me $35 per month—and, more importantly, provided me with a set of wheels.

I never got to go to college because my father became ill when I was in high school. I went to work in his construction business. I had an older sister who joined the convent and an older brother who had just entered the military. As third in line, I had to work to help feed and educate my eight younger siblings. I'm proud to say that all of them have degrees or multiple degrees. I'm the only one who doesn't have a formal education, and yet, I think I received the best education of all from that so-called school of hard knocks.

Be Different!

Champions find unique ways to solve problems, and they challenge others to do the same. They approach situations differently than most other people do. When I competed in the finals of the 1978 World Championship of Public Speaking in Vancouver, British Columbia, I was the ninth speaker out of nine on the dais that day. Two profound things happened.

Jeff Young, the 1979 winner of the World Championship, also competed in 1978 against me in Toronto. He spoke before I did and used a quote that I was going to use in my speech. I realize it was just a coincidence, but I was beside myself.

If I used the same quote, I surmised some might perceive that I was copying Jeff, even though we had to write and send our speeches in well in advance to allow the judges to determine that we were not repeating a previous speech. We were required to write a totally new speech and send copies of the ones we had used on the climb to the world finals.

So I changed my speech on the spot and did not use the quote. To this day, no one knew that I extemporaneously changed the speech that August day in 1978. I learned I should quote myself more and others less.

The other thing I noticed was that every speaker stayed at the lectern. No one moved. It never occurred to me not to move, but from what I gathered, no one had ever moved from behind the lectern at a Toastmasters International finals competition. To my knowledge, there was no rule against it and I had already requested a lavaliere microphone.

To make a long story short, I won the competition that day and I believe it was because I had the courage to be different on the platform. I needed to stand out. I needed to capture the imagination of the judges and the audience.

An audience member came up to me afterward and begrudgingly offered his congratulations but advised me that "If I was judging today, you'd have gotten a big goose egg." I asked why and he simply stated, "You aren't supposed to move from behind that lectern."

"Boy, I am glad you were not a judge," I responded. I was later told by Toastmasters International Executive Director Terrance McCann that to his knowledge I was the first contestant in the history of the competition ever to move on the platform.

Is that why I won? I don't know. All I know is this: If you want to be a champion, *you have to think differently.*

When you take care of your customers in a creative way, they will remember how you solved their problem and will reward you by letting others know. Unfortunately, that news is traveling half as fast as the bad news.

TAKEAWAY SERVICING AND SELLING TACTICS

1. Happy customers will share the good news but it only moves at half the speed of the bad news.
2. Develop good listening habits based on solid values.
3. Communicate, communicate, communicate. Nothing makes an unhappy customer angrier than someone who won't respond to their problem.

CHAPTER 27

BAD NEWS TRAVELS
AT THE SPEED OF LIGHT

*In the old days, they told a neighbor
or two. Today, it's the Internet that will
let the world's neighbors know just
how bad it really was.*

It's the Internet that will let the world's neighbors know just how great—
or terrible—their experience with your company really was. There are
no secrets anymore. You might as well think of the Internet as a gigantic
confessional and consider the world your confessor.

When you screwed up in the old days, the unhappy customer told a
couple of neighbors and called the Better Business Bureau. Today, they
tell a couple of million neighbors in a couple of hundred countries.
There's no place to hide.

The most wonderful thing about the Internet is that it puts the world
at your doorstep. The most maddening nightmare you'll ever face is
living down the bad news that spreads like wildfire to your digital doorstep. Now that the World Wide Web floodgates have been opened, you
can't poke a finger in the dike and hope to stop the leak. The damage
is done before you can blink an eye. And legitimate or not, there is no
governor on the web; people can say or allege anything they wish.

179

Businesspeople today have to do everything—sell, inform, update customers, solve problems—better and quicker than ever before. And although you can do very little about the toothpaste that's already out of the tube, you can—and must—control what is still in it.

Whether it's a grocery store advertising sale items that it conveniently doesn't have in stock or giant merchandisers that require you to complete a five page form to get your quarter back from a jammed gumball machine, the list of horror stories could fill the Library of Congress. The proliferation of technology allows these disgruntled customers to collect data on lousy service via audio and video. They're posting it faster than you can possibly respond, and there's simply no place to hide anymore. And that's not just the legitimate complaints that deserve condemnation. It is also the millions of exaggerations that are multiplied via the Web.

Add to this the explosion of social media and you have more fires than you can possibly fight. It is simply impossible to respond, so all the more reason to get it right going in so you won't have to fix it on the back end.

You may not be social media-savvy; you may feel that it's not important for your business or industry. However, there's not an industry or company today for whom this trend *isn't* relevant. Denying its existence will not make it go away, nor will it help you master it. Even if *you* do not use it, many of your clients do and they're talking to one another about your service, both good and bad.

LEARN THE JARGON

Social media creates another interesting challenge for those who aren't tuned in to the jargon, abbreviations, and acronyms that have exploded into a method of communication. An entire new language has erupted like a volcano in the world of social media.

I'm a moron when it comes to tech stuff. When my sons gave me an iPod, I actually thought it was a transistor radio. I told them I could only get one channel on the darn thing but it was a great channel. Had all my favorite beach music on it and the really cool part was that whenever

I cut it off, it always came back on to the same song and there were never any commercials. Man, is that ever awesome?

Now comes my newest technological challenge: text messaging. The first recorded text message was sent in December of 1992. Before you're done reading this chapter, the total number of text messages sent will exceed the population of the United States. Twenty-four hours from now, they will exceed the population of the entire planet.

I don't get the hidden messages within text messages. (MEGO) My eyes glaze over when it comes to this stuff. Does anyone write in complete sentences anymore? Do people still talk to one another over the phone?

I realize I'm a (nOOb) newbie to the text message thing. So (?4U) I have a question for you and I'm not looking for (TMI) too much information. (B4) before text messaging, how did we manage to communicate?

The big challenge is figuring out all the acronyms. I can't wait until my four-year-old granddaughter, Ashley, gets a little older so I can ask her what all this #$%^& means. I'm trying to (T+) think positive here but I prefer to (SIT) stay in touch the old fashioned way . . . with e-mail and the telephone.

But even e-mail is like alphabet soup anymore. Yes, when one of my employees needs (SOS) help, all he needs to do is ask for help. What's with the (SOS) stuff? Help is only one letter longer. Of course, (SOS) could also stand for Son of Sam.

I promised my wife today I would (T:}T) think happy thoughts when I wrote this chapter, but I'm wondering if my (PEEPS) people who are reading this garbage understand all this stuff. Come on (d00d), get with it. Why not just spell dude? I can understand that.

(NIGI) now I get it. I'm almost 62 and this is a language I just don't understand. I keep saying to myself (WIIFM) what's in it for me? I have to keep a text message manual around to understand what the sender is saying. (RTMS) read the manual stupid. (TA) thanks a lot. (WTG) Way to go . . . screw up my entire life by making me learn a new language. I'm too old and grumpy for this nonsense. I feel like telling them (MYOB) mind your own business. (OMG) Oh my God . . . (NSISR) not sure I spelled that right.

Kids love this stuff. They can communicate in code to keep their parents in the dark. For instance, (P911) clearly gives the receiver a heads-up that the parents are coming into the room. You could also go with the old standby (PAW) parents are watching. You have to give your (PEEPS) a heads-up. Can't have the older generation knowing what's between your ears. (GF) God forbid!

I want these kids to know I'm onto them. (TA) Thanks a lot. You can no longer get one by this old geezer. I might be (SQ) square, but I got my trusty text message glossary close by and it's (AWESO) awesome, which is how every kid under 18 describes everything today. What's that about? How can everything be (AWESO)?

I suspect I might be (ZZZZ) putting you to sleep with all this gibberish. Personally, I have (ZOT) zero tolerance for all this. (YYSSW) *yeah, yeah, sure, sure, whatever*, you say. You could have just said what every kid under 18 says (W/E) whatever and saved a few letters. But no, (UGTBK) you've got to be kidding; you have to pontificate with the *yeah, yeah, sure, sure* crap.

(UNBLEFBLE) unbelievable! What I really feel like saying is (^URS) up yours with all this acronym stuff. (BM) Bite me. (STFU) Shut the freak up.

(TTFN) Ta-ta for now. (CUL8R) See you later. Have a good (W/E) weekend. (ENUF) Enough already! I'm (1AM) one angry man. The last one's on me.

TAKEAWAY SERVICING AND SELLING TACTICS

1. Thanks to the Internet, the good news about great service is traveling faster. The bad news is traveling at the speed of light.
2. Get with the world of the social media and realize it's not going to go away.
3. Manage your business correctly going in and you won't have to clean up the mess coming out.

CHAPTER 28
NINE RULES THAT DRIVE CLIENT LOYALTY

RULE 1

"To lead the best, you have to be the best!"

Great customer-driven leaders manage the attention they give to others, and they manage the meaning of that attention. They control the level of trust that exists between themselves and others, and most importantly, they manage themselves. These leaders are always proactive; they are goal setters who begin with an end in mind. They know what they want the outcome of their actions to look like because they've envisioned it from the start. It's as clear as if they have already achieved it. They abide by the words of Henry Ford: "Whether you think you are successful or not, you're probably right either way."

Successful leaders always put first things first and clearly adopt the philosophy "What's the most important thing I can be doing right now?" They recognize the difference between important and urgent tasks at hand.

RULE 2

"Customer-driven leaders keep the axe sharpened and they listen."

Great leaders take the time to stay on top of their game.

RULE 3

"Customer-driven leaders make their team members' goals their own."

Great leaders serve as both the messenger and the message of what is important to those whom they guide. They are the example of what good behavior in the leadership arena should look like. While they envision goals for themselves, they are careful to make their people's goals part of their own. They let their people define those goals and take ownership of them.

Customer-driven leaders enjoy the process of motivating people to move to a higher plane. While communication skills are the primary factor, quality leadership is about managing our own behavior better so that others can define their parameters by our own. When we are in charge of our own management, we have ourselves to answer to.

Leadership is also about explaining the job properly and letting the troops know what is needed to "cover the nut." When a rat leaves the ship, it is usually because it is sinking.

Good leaders are a symbol of what their organization is all about. Their values are clear and their decisions come easy. Their thoughts represent the entire group's well-being. Most importantly, great leaders constantly renew their relationships with their people.

RULE 4

"Customer-driven leadership is about integrity and honesty."

Great customer-driven leadership, most importantly, is about integrity and honesty, and requires absolute competence on the part of the leader. It requires someone who is forward thinking, who can inspire and motivate the troops. And, most importantly, it requires intelligence.

THESE GREAT LEADERS ASK THE QUESTIONS:
- What's in the best interest of the majority?
- How can I keep people informed?
- How can I keep people involved?
- How can I run a meeting where we can agree to disagree?
- How can I become a better, proactive listener?

Our agency training tells our salespeople that if they're talking more than 20 percent of the time during discussions with clients, then they're talking too much.

Great customer-driven leaders expect to get results in real time, and have figured out how to beat the curve. They have mastered self-management through self-mastery: doing the things they are best at and letting others do what they're best at.

Most importantly, great leadership is about course correction. "When the horse is dead, get off of it," observed the late great speaker, Rosita Perez, CPAE Speaker Hall of Fame. Know when to change the direction—and more importantly, know *why* you're doing so.

RULE 5

"Customer-driven leaders know that goals sometimes change."

The difference between managing and leading can be described in the old adage : You manage *things*; you lead *people*. And leading people always requires some degree of flexibility. Leaders occasionally have to do things that they may not fully support. However, they recognize that you don't have to agree with a goal to achieve it; you just have to understand it. They're aware that while goals should be set based on the highest standards, they should also always leave room for improvement. Something that was considered to be the objective at the beginning of a process may not always be the aim at the end, or midway through. Leaders acknowledge this and "roll with the punches." They remain adaptable and take the action that best supports their people.

RULE 6

"Customer-driven leaders don't have to apologize for being successful."

If you don't make a profit, you won't have a business. If you don't lead people correctly, you won't keep them around. People must learn to stop apologizing for being successful, and for seeking to make a profit in business. One of the critical elements about good leadership is having people who bring hope to the people they are leading.

RULE 7

"Customer-driven leaders use their imaginations."

The unfair advantage in leadership occurs when leaders adjust to what happens while they're making other plans. Leaders must be change merchants and produce new ideas with an open mind and full heart. Effective leadership requires divergent thinking, the ability to withhold judgment until all the facts are in, and the ability to accept and understand the issues at hand.

Divergent thinking is an outward expansion of ideas from a narrow focus to a wide focus, from a narrow view to a broad view. This kind of imagination figures heavily into the leaders' decision processes. Thinking creatively is not an option; it is a requirement. It requires the ability to conceive something beyond the realm of one's immediate experience. In fact, great leaders even tend to operate better when an opportunity disguised as a problem does appear.

The salespeople in my agency have shown significant skill in dealing with objections. When there are no objections, they face their most difficult selling challenge—because they don't know the problem that needs to be addressed. This is when they regain control by asking questions and thinking creatively.

RULE 8

"Customer-driven leaders love to brainstorm."

Leaders who learn early in their tenure that brainstorming is one of the most important things they can do to move new ideas along mature much faster than the folks who have to learn that lesson the hard way. Brainstorming's purpose is to produce an abundance of new ideas to address a particular issue; to that end, it's vital to withhold judgment during the brainstorming process. Though quality does count, that can come later in the process. Effective brainstorming is about quantity of ideas first and quality of ideas later. Some good rules for brainstorming:

- Say everything that comes to mind.
- Permit no discussion, just ideas.
- No judging allowed (positive *or* negative).
- Repetition is okay.
- Piggybacking on others' ideas is encouraged.
- Accept and permit moments of silence.
- Bring closure at an appropriate point.

Leaders also permit *idea fluency* in that they prod the troops to think up a new way to address an old problem. One popular way to approach an issue is to simply ask, "How would you decide on this issue if you knew you couldn't fail?" That gives participants permission to think outside the box.

Another tool used in the brainstorming process is the *forced association* approach where the leader deliberately combines desperate ideas to get a novel result.

RULE 9

"Customer-driven leadership is a learned art form."

If we've learned anything about customer driven leadership, it is this: LEADERSHIP IS A LEARNED ART FORM.

Leaders can't pass along that which they don't already possess; no one can teach something that they don't know themselves. For that reason, leadership is empty unless one is committed to the process of learning. There are five important steps to the process to taking possession of an idea:

1. Attentively hearing, writing, reading, and saying the material.
2. Repeating it six times to produce about 62 percent retention.
3. Consciously making yourself use the techniques.
4. Internalizing the idea until it becomes part of your personality.
5. Reinforce by going back to basics once a month.

Like any art form, leadership is not just about doing the right things; it's about doing the right things *right*. Many of these so-called "right things" go directly to the issue of how the leader inventories his or her "idea shelf" with things that work.

CHAPTER 29

EIGHT RULES TO OVERCOME FEAR OF FAILURE

RULE 10

"The single greatest destroyer of customer-driven leaders is fear."

My grandfather once informed me that "Fear is nothing but an absence of knowledge [and] a lack of information."

Fear does indeed destroy leaders more than any other single factor. There are many times when our people are afraid of *us*—when they fear making a mistake and being forced to pay for it at a later point by getting fired. Sometimes their fear is based on misinformation; other times, it's based simply on prejudice.

People don't buy new ideas; they take ownership of them when they remove the fear with an abundance of knowledge.

RULE 11

"Customer-driven leaders are good at rapport building."

The most successful leaders have mastered the art of building rapport with their people. They are always seeking common ground. They know that the best way to be liked is to establish camaraderie and a shared sense of purpose with the other person. They do this by asking questions that give them insight into their team members' goals, passions, likes, and challenges.

Leaders always approach others in neutral. They know that if one dominant personality challenges another, they're heading for a war. To that end, they don't fight to "right"; instead, they figure out how to meet in the middle. They use noncontroversial topics to establish solidarity with others. Most important, they let team members know, "I'm here for you. You are important to me."

Leaders always use some kind of introductory statement to help get the conversation rolling. They employ phrases like "Let me begin by thanking you in advance for the time we'll share today . . . ." Or "The purpose of my visit here today. . . ." These are what are called "bridging statements"—learn to bridge.

Leaders also understand how critical it is to mirror another person's pace and rate of speaking. If one person is zipping along at 100 miles per hour and the other is cruising at 20, the slower person is likely to be overwhelmed. Keep an eye on the conversation's speedometer, and get everyone going at the same speed.

RULE 12

"Customer-driven leaders take notes when listening to others."

One of the greatest compliments you can give to another person is to ask permission to take notes as they speak to you, because it shows that:

- You are interested in what they're saying.
- You want to record their thoughts for future action.

Great leaders can recall the most crucial parts of their conversations and meetings with others because they record the data as it is being shared. They also have the unique ability to give feedback when the statements are made to clear up misunderstandings. They do this by using comments like:

- "It's my understanding that you said. . . ."
- "If I understand you correctly. . .,"
- "Correct me if I'm wrong, but I heard you say. . . ."

Good listening is about helping other people become better communicators. So take the time to hear them out. Don't interrupt. Set aside problem issues and come back to them later.

Once you have the data, feed it back to them and ask them to elaborate. Use assurance statements like "As I understand it, this is . . ." or "Is this more important or this . . ." Once you've come to agreement on an issue, follow with "that settles that" and move along.

Leaders bring closure to communication issues.

RULE 13

"Customer-driven leaders are frequently found among common people."

Great customer-driven leaders often come from humble beginnings. Nothing could be further from the truth than the conclusion that you have to be born with a silver spoon to be a great leader.

One of the top life insurance organizations in the world did some extensive research on their top-producing agents. Nearly 20 percent of these top agents, who made six- to seven-figure annual incomes, came from what could be best described as "dysfunctional environments." "Dysfunctional" meant everything from broken homes, divorces, and orphanages to alcohol and drug abuse. Because of the hardships they endured early on, these high-achieving salespeople learned very early in life exactly how to be responsible for themselves. They also learned the more important lesson of how to care for others—which they apply to this day in the way that they thoroughly care for our clients.

Having been thrust into this environment at a very young age, many of these agents were forced to acquire solid, usable leadership skills early on. In some ways, they had a head start on those who came from more "functional" environments.

RULE 14

"Customer-driven leaders understand that the airplane always takes off in the wind."

Customer-driven leaders understand that life is full of adversity. They know that when the winds are the greatest, the plane always takes off facing the wind. The old saying goes that it isn't the direction of the wind; it's the angle of the sail. In other words: You can usually do very little about the things that happen to you in your life. It's not what happens to you that matters; it's what you do about it, and how you choose to respond to it.

The most successful people in the world don't necessarily *have* the best of everything; they simply *make* the best of everything. They recognize that life is a struggle, and occasionally even brag about all of the obstacles they have overcome. Leaders are proud of their accomplishments; that pride is one of their greatest sources of energy.

RULE 15

"Customer-driven leaders encourage subordinates to give feedback—even when it's negative."

One of the greatest gifts that any leader can give their people is permission to "talk back to the boss." Leaders who build effective companies have a passion for excellence and never apologize for wanting to be the best. They know that in order to improve, they have to find out the best way to do so by asking their team members—the people running the organization on a daily basis.

Leaders know that they need to treat people fairly, though not necessarily *equally*. Those who go beyond the call of duty and give more than the job demands separate themselves from the merely adequate—and should be recognized as such. Leaders develop maturity by experiencing enough to look carefully the second time into things about which they thought they were certain the first time. When we observe feedback from others that causes us to change course, we speak directly to the issue of the troops talking back to the boss, because change always comes from the bottom up—never the top down.

RULE 16

"Customer-driven leaders practice the platinum rule."

The great leaders don't practice the golden rule. The golden rule says do unto others as you would have them do unto you. Most people don't think much of themselves and if someone did unto them what they would do themselves, you'd have a pretty good fight on your hands.

The great leaders practice the platinum rule. "Do unto others as others would have you do unto them," says speaker, author, and trainer Dr. Tony Alessandra, CSP, CPAE, co-author of *The Platinum Rule*.

These rules are not a sacrifice; they are an investment.

RULE 17

"Customer-driven leaders meet trouble head-on."

One of the profound tragedies in business today is leaders' failure to make decisions and take action. In contrast, great leaders meet trouble head-on and never shy away from the struggle. They thrive on change and are very autocratic in their approach to counseling others and managing processes. They never question their initial decision, nor do they hesitate to change it if it is wrong. They welcome having people around them who will weigh the pros and cons of a situation.

CHAPTER 30

SIX RULES OF SERVICE-
DRIVEN LEADERSHIP

RULE 18

"Customer-driven leaders have a passion about their mission."

Leaders show passion for their mission: a goal for their group or company. They know that these statements must very specifically state the organization's purpose. Unfortunately, too many leaders spend an inordinate amount of time trying to find the way when they don't even know where they're headed. In the absence of a goal, any path will do.

Even when leaders veer from their stated goal, leaders are positive. Failure is the process by which we succeed.

RULE 19

"Customer-driven leaders have the stamina to get the job done."

One of the hallmarks of great leadership is the tenacity with which leaders embrace their role. That tenacity requires a fair amount of physical stamina to take on the challenge. New century customer driven leaders must be both good mental and physical examples to their people. After all, if someone lets himself go, then what right does he have to correct another's path?

Not only do these leaders keep themselves in good physical shape, but they also keep themselves in great mental shape. Many read several magazines and newspapers per day and a book per week. They are constantly inquiring about new ways to solve old problems. Leaders know that building the stamina to accomplish their tasks takes cares of half the battle. Indeed, great leaders enjoy the journey almost as much as the destination.

RULE 20

"Customer-driven leaders focus on the positives and minimize the negatives."

Good leaders focus on positives. While they don't ignore the negatives, they do minimize and departmentalize it.

RULE 21

"Customer-driven leaders give value first."

"What I do best is share my enthusiasm."
—Bill Gates

I believe that Bill Gates would do what he does for free (but he certainly doesn't want people knowing that!) because he was simply more interested in creating better software than he was in becoming a multibillionaire. He is customer driven. The enthusiasm that is rampant across his organization begins with Gates himself and is passed along to everyone else. It's nearly impossible to imagine a company like Microsoft without a sense of enthusiasm driving every single decision. Gates' vision is part of his enthusiasm—and that vision constantly changes.

Gates doesn't hesitate to revise his objective at a moment's notice. For example, Gates revisited the goals he had set for Microsoft in the mid-nineties and turned the company 180 degrees from one path to another—all because his vision had changed. Leaders never see a project for the profits, but rather for the value they can bring to it, and the value it will provide to their customers.

Gates's loyalty to his team and respect for them as individuals is widely known. He gets respect by giving it first and understands that great leaders pass the torch.

RULE 22

"A customer-driven leader's strength lies solely in their tenacity of purpose."

Theodore Roosevelt once said, "Far better it is to have dared mighty things, to win glorious triumphs, even though checked by failure, than to take rank with those poor spirits who neither enjoy much nor suffer much. For they live in a gray twilight that knows neither victory nor defeat."

Tenacity of purpose is courage under pressure. A good question to ask: "How would I act if I knew I couldn't fail?"

One of the main reasons why people join Toastmasters is they understand that they cannot improve their tenacity in areas of communication if they don't get some practice. Toastmasters allow you to come together on a weekly basis and work on your "tenacious" skills.

Confidence comes from knowing that you know. You gain that when you participate in a Table Topics session at Toastmasters.

There's a sign on the gridiron at West Point that says, "On these friendly fields of strife are sown the seeds that on other fields and other days are borne the fruits of victory." On the friendly fields of Toastmasters are sown the seeds that on other platforms on other days are borne the fruits of great presentations.

RULE 23

"Customer-driven leaders believe the cost of experience is minimal as it is the best teacher."

There's an old German expression that says: "Your first loss is your least loss." Cut your losses and move on.

There is a distinct and measurable cost for taking or failing to take action. Sometimes we're better off taking the loss up front and moving to the next opportunity. Great leaders know when to cut their losses and move on. It's all tied to their mission statement and their purpose for being. Every experience, good or bad, should be a learning opportunity.

CHAPTER 31

FIVE RULES THAT DRIVE CUSTOMER ACHIEVEMENT AND SUCCESS

RULE 24

"Customer-driven leadership is about helping people make some memories."

One of the hallmarks of effective leaders is that they see their role as one that is constantly unfolding. You have to constantly adjust to market conditions, the economy, and all other considerations that go into your day-to-day dealings with customers.

RULE 25

"If you're coasting, you're heading downhill."

One of the big misconceptions about any customer-driven leadership position is that you can get to a point where you can coast. Coasting is never an option for a leader. Efficient leaders are continuously looking for ways to build a better mousetrap. They constantly question the status quo, rather than accepting it as the reality of the situation.

People often decide to coast at the expense of making a decision. In essence, coasting is about not being able to decide—even though "no decision" is still a decision.

You can't judge a leader by the number of times they made a bad decision, nor the number of times they made a good one. Success or failure should be measured in direct proportion to the number of times they fail and keep trying.

RULE 26

"Great customer-driven leaders are patient and reflective for reasons of self-preservation."

There is an old Arabic proverb that says, "If you are patient in one moment of anger, you will escape a hundred days of sorrow." Good leaders know this—and those who jump to conclusions often regret their reactions a short time later. It's perfectly fine to vent your frustrations both verbally or in writing; however, effective leaders know that they should ideally do this by themselves, in the privacy of their own office.

A rule that successful leaders live by: Make sure you give yourself 24 to 48 hours to evaluate your choice of words. Revisit the recording or printed document a day or two later to see if you still feel the same way about the issue. Evaluating your decision is more objective. You might want to soften it or strengthen it, but at least you can now approach it more objectively.

RULE 27

"Customer-driven leadership is a lot like love— you either have two winners, or none."

Leaders who love the people they lead are infinitely further along than those who simply tolerate others. In fact, perhaps the most important thing a leader can do for his troops is to love the profession of which they are both a part and always do the right thing. Sometimes the best thing you can do for a troop member is to help them find a new profession if this one isn't suited to them.

RULE 28

"Customer-driven leaders don't just look for the right people; they become the right people."

It's certainly not fair to expect to give away what you don't own. If your company sells widgets for a living, as their leader, you should be one of the best widget salespeople there are. You don't have to be the best, but in order to help others learn how to sell your product, you should at least have walked that path.

One of my big complaints about the speaking profession is that there are lots of speakers out there giving talks on topics with which they have no personal experience. They've never sold, yet they speak on selling. They've never run a company, yet they want to tell other people how to run theirs.

Our company subscribes to the highest standards and we expect no less of our people. We not only have to seek to hire the best people, we must first seek to *be* the best people. Only when you improve yourself can you improve others. Our leaders would not dream of guiding their teams on a given scenario unless they had experienced it—or something very similar—themselves.

CHAPTER 32

CLIENT-DRIVEN LEADERSHIP IS ABOUT REMOVING ROADBLOCKS

RULE 29

"Leaders aren't afraid to take a big step if one is necessary—because you can't cross a river in two steps."

Professional speaker Joel Weldon, CPAE, is fond of saying, "You can eat an elephant if you'll do it one bite at a time." That is, even the biggest, most daunting projects are doable if we can break them down in more manageable steps. Successful leaders know how to compartmentalize issues and sort out projects one step at a time.

They are also aware of the fact that you can't possibly know every single step of a process in advance; sometimes, you simply have to go with the flow. For example, if you left Florida to drive to southern California and you wanted to make absolutely sure of every street, every turn, every stop, every obstacle . . . you probably would never even leave on such a trip. All the options would literally overwhelm you. On the other hand, if you proceeded on your trip a day at a time, a state at a time, even an hour at a time, the immediate choices would be clearer and you wouldn't find yourself so overwhelmed.

The goal is to isolate the decision, observe all your options, and choose the one that fits the situation best. And remember to take it all one step at a time.

RULE 30

"Customer-driven leaders don't see through others; they see others through."

Lou Holtz, the great college football coach, once made the observation that "When you need love the most is when you get it the least."

Life is that way. The great leaders understand this and they show the way for their people. When someone has made a poor choice, it's easy to take on the role of the autocrat and hammer the decision as being wrong and costly.

The complete opposite of that is to let people totally off the hook after a poor choice. This "let me rescue you" mentality will be greeted with more "please rescue me" behavior on the part of the people we're supposed to be leading. You always get the kind of behavior you reward.

The great leader sees them through; they don't see through them. The successful leader is like a coach. They give people choices and they let them suffer the consequence of a bad decision or enjoy the fruits of a good decision.

When someone chooses poorly, the counselor-style leader uses several key ingredients. First, they encourage the person by using empathy and understanding. "I can understand how and why you reached that decision," the counselor might say. "Perhaps I would have decided that way myself."

The second half of the formula is the "consequence of the bad decision." We can't let people walk free from bad choices. It will only help cultivate an environment where more bad choices will follow. People have to take responsibility for their decisions. Rescuing them is not the answer; seeing them through their bad choice is.

RULE 32   205

RULE 31

"Customer-driven leaders understand that evil triumphs temporarily but never conquers."

Yes, from time to time, people screw up. But temporary screw-ups aren't the end of the world.

The highest paid hitters in baseball history fail to hit safely in two of every three attempts at the plate. Yet they are the best of the best.

Life is much the same way. We fail much more often than we succeed. It comes with the turf. Whether it's medical science or the sales profession, a certain amount of frequent failure will always exist. We should assume it.

A man failed in business in 1831. He was elected to the Legislature in 1832. He failed again in business in 1833. He was defeated for the Legislature in 1834. His sweetheart died in 1835. He suffered a nervous breakdown in 1836. He was defeated for Speaker in 1838. He was defeated for Lector in 1840. Defeated for Congress in 1843. Elected to Congress in 1846. Defeated for Congress in 1848Defeated for Senate in 1855. Defeated again for Senate in 1858. And he was elected President of the United States of America in 1860.

If each of us had the tenacity of purpose, the commitment to a cause that Abraham Lincoln had, greater leadership would be the immediate by-product.

To paraphrase the great Indiana basketball coach Bobby Knight: "Everyone wants to be on a championship team, but nobody wants to come to practice." As the old saying goes, "Everybody wants to go to heaven, nobody wants to die."

RULE 32

"Customer-driven leaders make it a point to keep up pleasantly with bad news."

Baseball players keep statistics like they are prized possessions, and indeed they are. A pitcher's earned run average (ERA) is as critical to his success on the mound as it is in his bank.

When Nolan Ryan hurled one of his many no-hitters, he was quoted as saying "Just like practice." In practice, Ryan made it a point to keep up with the bad news. He made a mental note to himself to pitch this guy a certain way. Avoid high fast balls to that guy. He also kept himself in superb physical shape and he was able to compete into his 40s.

Another great baseball pitcher, Greg Maddux, always kept a chart on every hitter he's ever faced. He makes meticulous notes to himself about the hitter's tendencies and habits. It gives him the "unfair advantage."

While Ryan was a "blow-it-past-them" kind of a hurler and Maddux was more of a finesse player, the pair had similar earned run averages and proportionate wins on the baseball diamond. Both men knew that there was negative in every positive and positive in every negative. Just knowing that allows you to "keep up pleasantly with the bad news."

CHAPTER 33

SIX RULES THAT DRIVE CLIENT RESULTS

RULE 33

"Leaders understand that the higher the risk, the more likely the casualties—and the more satisfying the reward."

Today's leadership is about understanding the risks involved in making key decisions—both everyday choices and critical judgments with potentially long-term consequences. Businesspeople consider the risk that's involved in their business. Since risks present situations where money can be potentially gained or lost, most know to tread carefully. Generally, a bigger risk means a bigger reward—but when you swim in the deep water, you have to know the rules. "People who fight fire with fire usually end up with ashes," wrote Abigail Van Buren. You must know the cost of the risk.

RULE 34

"Customer-driven leaders understand that activity leads to aptitude."

Leaders encourage their team members to get as much exposure and experience as possible, and to track their successes and failures. The more they do, the more they learn. We believe in keeping score in our agency; to that end, our agents file a number of reports each week that track several things:

1. How many clients did the agent actually speak to this week?
2. How many gave the agent an appointment?
3. How many purchased something?
4. What was the value of the appointment (divide income by number of appointments)?
5. What was the value of each phone call (divide income by number of phone calls)?

When you approach your efforts this way, you understand that even a "no" has value. Every time someone told the agent to "take a hike," the agent still made "$X" regardless of the outcome of the sale.

A sophisticated customer-driven leader will measure activity, and achievement takes care of itself. Control the activity and you control the achievement.

RULE 35

"Customer-driven leaders understand that the time to fix the roof is when the sun is shining."

One of the nicest things about measuring activity is that you get a head start on the problems that lie ahead. When I check my agents for the number of calls they made, I want to know if the effort was made to reach a respectable number of people. If an agent is closing only 20 percent, this is a telltale sign that something is wrong. Did the agent cultivate his market correctly? Did he send out enough pre-approach mail? Did he choose the best candidates to purchase his product? Monitoring activity can quite accurately predict future behavior.

We teach our agents to send 30 pre-approach letters per week to potential clients. Skipping this step essentially ensures that your phone ratio will dip significantly the following week. However, 30 letters won't get the job done unless you make 30 phone calls to those people *for appointments*. If you want 15 appointments per week, then you should either have a 50 percent closing ratio on the phone or you might have to phone more people. You have to keep adding wood to the fire, or it will go out.

RULE 36

"Customer-driven leaders know which bridges to burn and which bridges to cross."

While some say the first loss is the smallest loss, others would argue that occasionally you have to burn a bridge and move along. It's not worth garnering anything from the relationship. The time and effort we put into personal relationships must show a respectable return or we're better off minimizing the relationship altogether. The customer isn't always right, but they are always the customer . . . unless you fire them.

RULE 37

"Customer-driven leaders form the right habits."

"Success is a habit. Winning is a habit. Unfortunately, so is losing."
—*Vince Lombardi, Hall of Fame football coach*

Any person's strengths, overused, can become their weaknesses. If you've folded your arms the same way for most of your life, you're not likely to automatically reverse that fold unconsciously. If you fold your fingers a certain way, it's not likely that you will unconsciously move them down a digit.

Habits are just as difficult to establish as they are to break. Try the arm folding or hand folding exercise. Reverse the fold of the arms or move your fingers to a different notch. You immediately experience discomfort. That discomfort is all about change. We resist it. We fight it.

Conversely, if you make a conscious habit to fold your arms or hands a new way, and if you do it for 17 of the next 21 days, social scientists suggested that you have now displaced your old behavior with the new behavior.

If a person does not wear a seat belt, they may feel confined in one. People who are in the habit of using a seat belt would never get into another vehicle again without one. Both the bad habit of not wearing the belt and the good habit of wearing one are driven by previous behavior, beliefs, rules, and occasionally the law.

Only when we become disturbed by our old behavior will we displace that activity with new activity. Change comes only when we feel uncomfortable with the previous behavior.

RULE 38

"Customer-driven leaders are up early and stay late."

If you want your dreams to come true, don't oversleep. Customer driven leaders realize that they don't have a part-time or "sometimes" job. It is, in fact, an "all-the-time job."

Leaders get up early and work late. It is simple as that. There's no free lunch when it comes to the time necessary for the leader to survive. Work ethic is something that people bring to a position. You either have it or you don't. As a leader, you can't coach "want to" in other people— they have to bring that to the table themselves.

"Want to," however, can be an acquired trait—if the person who wants to has enough desire and discipline. It requires a clearly defined mission statement that includes very specific ideas on who, what, when, where, why, and how one approaches a challenge.

When I hire new people, I look for those who worked or were care-givers during their youth. I find that some of the very best salespeople in the world had to do a lot of work at an early age—whether it was tak-ing care of a sick parent or working and putting money into the family pot each week. These people learned responsibility early, and it stuck with them.

I was the third of 11 children born to the late Alice C. and Michael A. Aun Sr. I worked hard in my youth.

At age 5, I began bagging groceries in my grandfather's grocery store and later in my uncle's stores.

By the time I was 9, I was delivering newspapers by bicycle over a route that was about 20 miles long.

By age 12, I was pumping gas and changing oil for customers of Ralph Corley's Exxon Station on Main Street, Lexington, South Carolina. I worked 80 to 90 hours per week during the summer for $1.00 per hour, which I turned over to my mother each week. This was not a normal functioning environment.

By age 16, I was a stringer for a half-dozen newspapers in the central South Carolina area.

By age 17, I was writing for a half-dozen newspapers, working part-time at the service station and driving a school bus, all of which gener-ated income. I'm now syndicated in over 600 newspapers and electronic publications in 22 countries throughout the world.

I have found that the work habits I developed during my youth have profoundly affected my ability to achieve as an adult. A leopard doesn't change its spots.

The great customer-driven leaders of the next century will be people who know that you must pay a price in terms of time to succeed, and who are aware that there are simply no shortcuts. Once in awhile, peo-ple get lucky, but on balance, you pay a distinct and specific price to be successful as a leader.

According to H.L. Hunt of the Kansas City Chiefs, there are only two issues regarding reaching your goals in life:

1. Find out what you want out of life.
2. Determine what you have to give up for it.

In most cases, these steps involve time and stamina. There's no question that great leaders get up early and stay late. They usually sleep no more than six hours per night. They generally exercise to keep their stamina. Ideally, they don't abuse their bodies with food, alcohol, drugs, or other lack of rest.

And they play as hard as they work. If you don't take a vacation, God will give you one—so work hard, and rest hard, too.

CHAPTER 34

TEN RULES THAT DRIVE CLIENT DECISIONS AND LOYALTY

RULE 39

"Customer-driven leaders understand that you can't shake hands if your fists are balled."

A significant part of leadership is the ability to compromise when it's appropriate. If you're all hot and bothered over a situation, compromise is difficult to achieve. After all, you can't shake hands if your fists are balled.

One must question the standards by which compromise is being achieved. What is the minimum acceptable standard that you can identify? How can you give a little, but get a little, too? If you can meet another person halfway on just a few issues, you'll open the fist and that will open your heart to settling the issue.

RULE 40

"Two rules of customer-driven leadership:
Rule # 1 . . . don't quit.
Rule # 2 . . . see Rule 1."

Great customer-driven leaders have a low tolerance level for quitting—for themselves, and for others. It's not in their vocabulary to quit. It's simply not an option. They never see it as an option in others, either.

The old saying "A winner never quits and a quitter never wins" is pretty good advice. The man or woman who simply loses just ran out of time. The person who quits defeats himself or herself.

Quitting, simply put, should never be an option. Leaders who are responsible take this into consideration and refuse to veer. They also refuse to allow the people on their watch to quit.

Rule 41

"Customer-driven leaders know the difference between a bend in the road and the end of the road."

Twenty-first century leaders are always two steps ahead of the rest of the group. They know that every road has a bend in it, and they also know that simply because there's a bend doesn't mean it will end.

Ironically, people have come to accept that less than the best, while not okay, has become the standard. Exceptional customer service has become more about accepting mediocrity than achieving excellence.

Winning leaders understand there is going to be a bump in the road and more than one bend along the way. They walk the path first so they can be prepared to lead others down it. That is what gives them the right to call themselves a leader. The end of the road is when one or both sides are in a no-win situation.

Rule 42

"Great customer-driven leaders take the heat when it's someone else's fault."

Great leaders take the heat for their people from time to time. They know that while there's some stuff you pass along to the troops, there's some you just have to swallow yourself. They make this call based on the situation at hand. While they know that it's best to pass praise along publicly, they should deal with the heat—the errors and blame—privately, and in a caring fashion. Great leaders take the blame when necessary and they always work with their people to fix the problem instead of harping on who's to blame.

RULE 43

"Great customer-driven leaders are more interested in being faithful than famous."

One of the most admirable attributes of 21st century leaders is their faithfulness to their companies, customers, and the people on their team. For several decades now, the loyalty issue has become less and less a factor from the employees' standpoint. While many people born during the Depression worked in one industry for their entire life, people are "job hopping" more and more frequently these days. A leader knows when his team members are a perfect fit, and when to encourage them to continue on their path.

RULE 44

"Customer-driven leaders understand that some days you're the steamroller and some days you're the road."

The bumper sticker (or at least the abbreviated version) says ". . . it happens!" Things do happen—and in most cases, we have little control over the stuff that goes on in our lives. Some days you're doing the steamrollering, and some days you're the road.

It's not what happens to you that matters very much, but how you react to it! Many of us go through our lives spending an inordinate amount of time on two things: WORRY and REGRET. Most of the stuff we worry about never comes to pass. Worry, after all, is the price we pay in advance for something that has less than 1 chance in 10 of happening.

Regret can be even *more* destructive. One hundred percent of the things we regret can never be changed. They are yesterday's news—gone forever. That's not to suggest that we shouldn't learn from our history. On the contrary, we should go to great pains to grow and develop from everything we do.

However, sometimes things happen—and we can't do a single thing about them. We're stuck with the hand we're dealt.

Singer/actress Dolly Parton put it best: "You can't have the rainbow without the rain."

RULE 45

"Customer-driven leaders do get mad, but they get over it."

The leader who has never lost his or her temper just hasn't been leading long enough! The effective leader consciously knows how to channel their anger to produce maximum results.

Leaders know that in order to settle these occasional misunderstandings, they need to isolate them. Here are the keys:

- Determine problem.
- Isolate it in simplest terms.
- Consider all possible solutions.
- Give all parties a voice.
- Make the best decision.

Never let borderline issues crop up in dealing with your or someone else's anger. Restrict the discussion to the issue at hand and refuse to allow peripheral issues to crop up. This will help you control both other people's anger and your own, to make sure that the problem you set out to solve gets the attention it deserves.

RULE 46

"Customer-driven leaders don't let conflicting facts prevent a decision from being reached."

Sometime we have to play King Solomon and offer to "split the baby." Every leader has had occasion to face issues involving conflicting facts. While that's not unusual, letting these issues prohibit the leader from reaching a decision is unacceptable. A good leader recognizes and addresses the conflict and makes a choice in spite of it.

The flip side of this is when there is no conflicting evidence *whatsoever*—a definitively less desirable scenario. It's far better to have people who will "talk back" to the boss and get some healthy debate brewing than to have a bunch of "yes people" who are only concerned with protecting their turf and not stirring the pot.

The old saying, "If we agree on everything one of us isn't needed," is very appropriate here. There certainly doesn't need to be confrontation in every situation, but often, it provides us with ways to improve.

RULE 47

"Customer-driven leaders share credit."

If you spread the blame, you must share the credit as well. Great leaders find a way to put their people in the picture when it comes time to enjoy a victory. When distributing praise, they consider the following:

- Do it at an appropriate time and place.
- Choose the venue to maximize your return.

- Be very specific as to how the team member(s) helped.
- Make sure that you slight no one.

Giving credit to others actually says more about you than it does about them. In the speaking business, a standing ovation is not always the hall-mark of a great presentation. Many audiences give that kind of feedback simply because they view it as good behavior on their own part.

Give credit where credit is due and be responsible about it. It should have been earned, because nothing is more insincere than undeserved flattery. Those who are victims of it are as embarrassed as the people who know the true story.

When giving credit to others, follow these guidelines:

- Do it quickly. (Delaying can minimize the benefit.)
- Keep it short. (Overkill can minimize the gain.)
- Be specific. (Let them know exactly why their efforts helped.)
- Do it personally. (Don't delegate important tasks like rewarding good behavior.)

RULE 48

"Customer-driven leaders bring hope to others."

It's been said that a man can live about 40 days without food, about three days without water, and about eight minutes without air . . . but only one second without hope.

The great leaders of the 21st century are those who have and share hope. Their vision in their business is built on a foundation of hope. Their hope for tomorrow is not about profits, but about building a better widget. They know that the profits will come when better widgets are built. They live not for yesterday or today, but for tomorrow, ever-optimistic and ever-vigilant. Hope to them is a pilot that steers them safely along life's path, always following their mission and dream. It's an ever-changing feeling that you can improve on success, but more important, it allows the thoughtful leader to understand how to deal with today's frustrations.

Some people are perceived as "overly" optimistic. Great leaders measure their optimism and understand that any excess of hope might be a medicine to another who is despondent. They work to pull others up a level.

Great leaders understand that their health is important and their hopes are pinned on their well-being. Many of these same leaders feel that it is important to do the impossible, that there are no hopeless situations. They understand that one can become bankrupt in hope as well as in business. While hope consists of many ingredients, the most important are courage, hard work, a will to win, and solid faith. These leaders see hope like the sun, which, as we journey toward it, casts the shadow of our burden behind us.

Leaders who perish are those who have lost their vision and their ability to dream. They've lost their ideals, the very things that helped them to come as far as they've come. They've lost heart and hope. Without that nucleus, all life comes to an end. Today's leaders will believe as Clare Boothe Luce believed: "There are no hopeless situations; there are only hopeless men."

ABOUT THE AUTHOR

Michael Aun has been speaking professionally since 1974 when he began his career in the insurance business with the Knights of Columbus. His General Agency spans multiple offices throughout central Florida, servicing some 35,000 policyholders in over 100 cities. He holds the FIC and LUTCF designations in the insurance industry. He has been a Qualifying Member of the Million Dollar Round Table and has addressed that prestigious body.

Michael Aun is the author of seven books. His syndicated column "Behind the Mike" appears in over 600 newspapers and electronic publications in some 22 countries in several languages.

In 1978, Michael Aun won the World Championship of Public Speaking for Toastmasters International, an organization of some 175,000 members in over 60 countries at the time.

In 1983, Michael Aun earned his Certified Speaking Professional (CSP) designation from the National Speakers Association, one of only 200 in the world at that time. He has also been elected to NSA's Board of Directors.

In 2000, he was inducted to the CPAE Speaker Hall of Fame, an award widely recognized as the Oscar of the speaking profession by the National Speakers Association. He is also a member of the Toastmasters International Speakers Hall of Fame.

In 2003, he was presented the prestigious George Morrissey Lifetime Achievement Award by the Central Florida Speakers Association.

In 2009, he was decorated by the Veteran Speakers Conference as a recipient of the Legends of the Speaking Profession Award. He is one of only 67 speakers to be so honored over their history and was the youngest ever selected. Forty-two honorees are still alive.

Michael and his wife, Christine, reside in St. Cloud, Florida, and are the parents of three sons. He can be reached at P.O. Box 701385, St. Cloud, Florida 34770-1385 or through his web site http://www .aunline.com/blog/.

INDEX